# OLD DORSET

# OLD DORSET

by

## M. B. WEINSTOCK

DAVID AND CHARLES
NEWTON ABBOT

7153  4174  ×

—

Printed in Great Britain by
Latimer Trend & Company Limited Plymouth
for David & Charles (Publishers) Limited
South Devon House  Railway Station
Newton Abbot  Devon

# Contents

# *Illustrations*

## PLATES

## *Illustrations*

### LINE DRAWINGS IN TEXT

# Introduction

The traveller in Dorset can see many signs of history all around him. Ancient man has left his memorials on many hilltops. Before the dawn of written history palaeolithic folk hunted in the river valley of the Frome, where their flint axes have been found in the gravel pits. Mesolithic men made their flint tools in the Purbecks. Later, prehistoric men buried their dead in the long barrows of Pimperne and Long Bredy and conducted their sacred rites in the Knowlton Circles near Wimborne or on the fringe of Dorchester. Standing clear along many hilltops are the round burial barrows of Bronze Age man; several stone circles stand also as his memorials.

In the Iron Age men began more regularly to cultivate the land. The small rectangular fields spread over the Dorset downlands. In the centre of the county, near Portesham and to the west of Lulworth Cove, these can be seen. More impressive still are the great camps, concentric rings of ditches with internal banks on which were placed palisades as additional defence. Eggardon, Hambledon, Badbury and Hod were once both thriving villages and strongholds in times of trouble. Maiden Castle, outside Dorchester, dominates the landscape and, seen in the evening light, is breathtaking in its splendour. The Castle has been carefully excavated, revealing details of the type of hut that Iron Age man built for himself. One of them, circular in plan, with a diameter of twenty-two feet, had a chalk wall with an inner circle of timber posts to support the roof. There were three clay ovens, originally dome-shaped, in the inner part of the hut. Later a new floor was laid over the ovens and a central hearth built thereon. A visit to Dorchester Museum will show the visitor many of the finds from this site; bead rim bowls and weapons. The visitor should also look at the Cerne Giant of Romano-British times, carved in the chalk of the hillside, possibly a fertility symbol. A great man straddles the hillside with his club in his hand.

The Romans knew Dorset well. They attacked Maiden Castle where the defenders died in battle. Later they built a temple there as elsewhere in the county. Some of their pavements lie open for the visitor to see. The complete foundations of one of their houses can be studied in Dorchester, and a marvellous stretch of Roman road runs from Badbury north to Old Sarum. In Dorset, too, the first English portrait of Christ has recently been discovered in a Roman pavement at Hinton St Mary. The mosaic is in the British Museum, but pictures of it can be seen in Dorchester. The great amphitheatre of Maumbury, outside the town, is beautiful in its perfection.

In 705, three centuries after the Romans left Britain, King Ine of Wessex made Sherborne a bishopric for St Aldhelm. He founded a line of learned and fighting bishops, some of whom fell in battle against the Danes. Famous among the scholar bishops was Asser, the biographer of King Alfred. Of Aldhelm's abbey church few signs remain. A doorway and a portion of wall were spared when the eighth-century building was pulled down in Norman times. Here Roger of Caen, bishop of Sarum, was to build anew; some of his pillars and walls and his great tower survive in the later medieval rebuilding of the abbey church after the jealous townsfolk had set fire to it with a flaming arrow.

Shaftesbury, too, has traces of a very early nunnery for Benedictine nuns. When the Abbey of St Mary the Virgin was founded by Alfred, his daughter became the first abbess. Today a fragment of a fine buttressed wall can be seen on the flank of Golden Hill, with other traces of what was once a magnificent group of buildings.

The Normans left their memorials in county churches and castle mounds, but an even more splendid monument of medieval history is enshrined in Woodsford Castle, near Dorchester. In 1368 Sir Guy de Bryan began to build a great fortified manor house which still remains, topped by one of the largest thatched roofs in the country. The original newel staircase, the chapel, solar, kitchen, guardroom and a square tower give some idea of its medieval splendour. This period of Dorset history is further reflected in the noble tithe barn at Abbotsbury, all that remains of what was once a great monastery; the lovely gatehouse and guest house at Cerne Abbas, where too, is a magnificent tithe barn, all date from the Middle Ages. At Toller Fratrum the Knights Hospitallers of St John of Jerusalem had obedientaries and were also linked with Forde Abbey. Some time after the dissolution, Inigo Jones, or his pupil John Webb, remodelled the buildings of Forde Abbey. Much the same thing happened to the Benedictine Abbey at Milton. Originally a Saxon foundation, the old buildings which remain were erected in the fourteenth century. John Tregonwell, one of the Commissioners for the surrender of the Abbey at the dissolution, bought it for £1,000. He was buried in the church. The Abbot's Hall, built in 1498, was preserved when the architect, Sir William Chambers, did much rebuilding later on.

Dorset abounds in beautiful small Tudor and Stuart manor houses. Athelhampton, Sandford Orchas, Cranborne Manor and Bingham's Melcombe are gems of this period. Creech Grange, Crichel, Encombe, old Kingston Maurward, to name only a few, show Dorset history in stone. Purse Caundle, Hammoon, Rampisham, Winterborne Anderton are all different, yet all beautiful in ham stone or brick and thatch. The Great Chamber of Purse Caundle Manor and the hall with the arch-braced collar beam roof speak clearly of old Dorset.

No attempt has been made in the chapters that follow to tell the story of the county in detail. In the main they deal with certain aspects of county activities or of people who made history, even briefly, in more recent times. From these simple accounts it is hoped that a picture of the life of the county will emerge. Wills and inventories, census returns, letterbooks, trade ledgers, registers, diaries and journals are some of the sources used. For easier reading, much of the spelling has been modernized, though a little has been kept to give the true flavour of the time. Paul Nash, writing of the face of Dorset, spoke of 'a gigantic face composed of massive and unusual features; at once harsh and tender, alarming yet kind, seeming susceptible to moods but, in secret, overcast by a noble melancholy—or, simply, the burden of its extraordinary inheritance. Indeed, the past is always evident in that face.' It is with a little of that past reflected in buildings and records that this book deals.

# CHAPTER ONE

## Some houses of the great and humble

*Corfe Castle*

In Saxon times a royal hunting lodge stood on the natural mound which made Corfe a great stronghold, one of the finest sites in the country. Purbeck was famous for its hunting. In 978 the young King Edward, having lost his attendants, rode alone to Corfe to his stepmother Elfrida for food. She was anxious that her own young son should succeed. The story goes that, as the King sat on his horse at the gate, the Queen's retainers thronged round him and her butler brought him out a horn of wine by way of welcome. While he was thus distracted one of the men suddenly grasped his right hand, pretending to kiss it, while another stabbed him mortally from behind. Edward fell dead from his horse; his body was buried, without full rites, at Wareham. A year later Alfhere of Mercia disinterred it, found it incorrupt, and gave it honourable burial at Shaftesbury. 'There has never been among the English a worse deed done than this, since they sought Britain', says the Anglo-Saxon Chronicle; 'his murderers would blot out his memory, but the Avenger on High has spread his fame in heaven and earth. Those who would not bow to his living body now humbly bend on their knees before his dead bones.' Remorse overcame Queen Elfrida, who eventually entered a nunnery. Corfe Church is dedicated to Edward the King and Martyr.

There is no mention of Corfe in Domesday, but during the reign of Henry I at the beginning of the twelfth century building in stone must have begun, since in 1139 the exiled Earl Baldwin de Redvers landed at Wareham, seized the Castle for Queen Matilda and held it against Stephen. Internal rebellions made it necessary to station large garrisons about the country, so two large baileys were added one after another to the castle, which became a royal stronghold and prison. Considerable sums were spent on the building. The Sheriff laid out twenty shillings in repairs in 1189 and twenty marks later in the reign. Expenditure in John's reign was larger still and ran into hundreds of pounds, work being done on the Castle under royal surveyors. Wood came in by sea, and miners and stonemasons were employed at threepence or sixpence a day.

John stayed at the Castle and kept the royal regalia there. There, too, he imprisoned his nephew Arthur, Duke of Brittany, and Eleanor his sister. With them were a number of French knights who had been loaded with fetters and 'huddled like calves' into carts for transport to English prisons. It is believed that twenty-two of these unfortunates, who had no friends to pay their ransoms, starved to death in the Castle. Eleanor was subsequently joined by two daughters of the King of Scotland, as hostages for their father. The Mayor of Winchester was ordered to send for their use 'robes of dark green, namely tunics and supertunics with capes of cambric and fur of minever, and twenty-three yards of good linen cloth'; a good dark brown fur cap and a hood for rainy days were needed, also bright green robes for the waiting-maids with rabbitskin caps and lambskin fur. All the ladies wanted their shoes and Eleanor needed a horse bridle. The Mayor was to come to Corfe with the clothing and there receive payment. Later Eleanor was to have a 'beautiful saddle with scarlet ornaments and golden reins'. Two pairs of boots were brought for her to use when the fur shoes would not be suitable. In 1221 Eleanor was taken from Corfe to Gloucester and thence to Marlborough and Bristol where she ultimately died.

In 1280 Edward I rebuilt Corfe Castle. The keep had the usual two storeys with a squarish hall, a wall beneath the centre of the span helping to support the floor, with a small chamber to the north. A special tower was constructed beside the hall for the latrines which discharged down the slope of the great mound. The amounts laid out by the Constable show how much work was undertaken.

Timber, lime, lead and stones were all bought. Tilers, masons, carpenters, blacksmiths and plumbers were busy. A permanent surveyor looked after them. The great tower rose. The prisons were cleaned out, three men and four women getting 12d for cleaning *Swalwe*, 5¼d for *Malemit*. Carts were hired, candles bought.

1. Corfe Castle

2. Gateway to Eastbury House

In one year, 1281–2, £98 8s 1d was spent. Then the painters began to beautify the buildings—6s 8d for whitewashing the royal chamber appears in the accounts.

Another unfortunate prisoner, Edward II, came to the Castle after his capture in 1326 by the barons. There was irony in the situation, since the King had sent some of his prisoners there during his reign. From Corfe Edward was escorted secretly by Sir John Matravers to Berkeley Castle and his death.

New buildings and repairs to old ones continued in successive reigns. When Edward III was expected, a hasty spring-cleaning had to take place; in the high tower the king's chamber and other rooms had rotten floorboards which had to be taken out quickly, horsemen riding to Dorchester to get nails for the new flooring. Rubbish had to be cleared away.

In later medieval times the Castle was held by the Earls of Kent and Somerset and George, Duke of Clarence.

Henry VII prepared the Castle for his mother, the Countess of Richmond. She knew and liked Dorset, since she had lived at Kingston Lacy, near Wimborne, as a little girl. When she died her grandson Henry VIII granted the Castle to one of his illegitimate children. The Lord Protector Somerset held it at one time. In Elizabeth's reign the Castle ceased to be a royal residence and was sold to Christopher Hatton for £4,761 18s 7½d. Hatton had no direct heirs, so the property passed to his nephew. Subsequently a Hatton widow married Sir Edward Coke the Attorney General, who was many years her senior. Left a widow for the second time, Lady Coke sold the Castle to Sir John Bankes of Kingston Lacy.

Now began the last and possibly the most illustrious chapter of the Castle's history. Shortly after the outbreak of the Civil War, Lady Bankes decided that the Castle would be the safest home for herself and her children. Her husband was with the Earl of Oxford. There was no garrison at the Castle; Lady Bankes had only five men and the women of the household. By May 1643 the Parliamentary forces were drawing near. Sir Walter Erle and Sir Thomas Trenchard had captured Dorchester, Weymouth, Lyme Regis, Wareham and Poole; Corfe Castle would be a valuable prize. An attempt was made by a band of troops to gain admittance on the plea of wanting to see over the Castle. Lady Bankes refused them entry and also a subsequent request to surrender four small cannon.

Thereupon a party of seamen from Poole appeared before the Castle demanding the guns. Lady Bankes replied by ordering one of them to be loaded and fired. The seamen retired. By beat of drum her tenants and friends were summoned and a guard was mounted. Threatening letters were received, insisting that if the guns were not given up the houses of her helpers might be fired. Some of the tenants, persuaded by their weeping wives, went home. Strict watch was kept in the Castle. A proclamation was made at Wareham that no food or drink should be sold to the Castle. Gunpowder sent to it was captured on the road. No one could get in or out. Under this pressure Lady Bankes agreed to surrender the guns if she were allowed to remain peacefully in the Castle.

There followed a lull, during which the lady furnished the Castle with food and gunpowder. Urgent messages were sent to the Royalist forces nearing Blandford that help was imperative. A small force under Captain Lawrence arrived. Again the Castle was called upon to surrender by a party of Parliamentary horse, who fired on the town from the encircling hills. Lady Bankes staunchly held out. Attempts were made to bribe some of the household servants. They were offered double pay and a share of the plunder of the Castle if they opened it to the besiegers, whose guns kept the buildings under fire. Siege weapons were constructed and pushed up to the walls, and the parish church became an observation post. Reinforcements of sailors armed with petards and scaling ladders arrived, but no man was brave enough to win a reward of twenty pounds by being the first to scale the walls.

The commanders then gave drink to their troops until they were 'pot-valiant and possessed of borrowed courage' and divided them into two parties to attack the middle and upper wards. While Captain Lawrence defended the middle ward, Lady Bankes with her daughters, serving women and five men, guarded the upper ward and 'did bravely perform what she undertook; for by heaving over stones and hot embers they repelled the rebels and kept them from climbing their ladders, thence to throw in that wild fire, which every rebel had in his hands'. The Parliamentary forces suffered heavy losses and, hearing that the Royalists were drawing near, Sir Walter Erle withdrew to Poole. The six-week siege of the Castle had ended, but only for the time being.

By August 1644 the Royalist fortunes were waning. Corfe stood as almost the sole stronghold between Devon and London. The country round was hostile. Lady Bankes and her children were proclaimed rebels and their property forfeit. At Christmas Sir John Bankes died away from home, and his widow had to face the future alone. In October 1645 began the second siege of the Castle by Colonel Bingham, Governor of Poole. The Royalist Colonel Pitman, of the Castle garrison, entered into an agreement that, given protection, he would turn traitor and arrange that Parliamentary troops should gain admittance. The plot succeeded; a sizeable force was allowed in under the mistaken belief that they were reinforcements. Treachery succeeded where direct assaults had failed. Lady Bankes had no option but to treat with Colonel Bingham, who spared the lives of the women within the Castle. Lady Bankes and her family went free but homeless.

A sad fate befell the Castle, which was blown up. The cost of destroying the massive medieval walls was undertaken by Captain Hughes, Governor of Lulworth Castle. His account for the work came to £368 9s od.

In recognition of her bravery Colonel Bingham allowed Lady Bankes to keep the keys of the Castle. She kept nothing more from it. The tapestries from the gallery and great chamber were taken by Colonel Bingham for himself; likewise an ebony cabinet and gilt hangings. His troops plundered thoroughly. Someone must have enjoyed wearing 'the crimson satin petticoat with a stomacher and sleeves lined with silver'. The loot was immense. In addition to the tapestry, there were green leather gilted hangings, blue silk silver-and-white hangings, quilted silk table covers, plush and damask hangings, 'French green cloth bed furnishings with changeable taffety tester head-cloth and fringe' and Indian white quilts, innumerable feather beds, bolsters, blankets, and down pillows with fine linen. There were Persian and Turkey carpets and crimson velvet chairs, stools, an embroidered couch and long cushions of crimson velvet. Poor Lady Bankes; her household linen marked N.B. or I.B., her children's linen, and many books and papers vanished, as did a very large trunk 'inlay'd all over with mother of pearle'.

Thus Corfe Castle stands 'a scene of havoc and desolation as strike every curious spectator with horror and concern'. A recent Government has made slight amends by a grant to help with the preservation of the ruins.

# Some houses of the great and humble

## Eastbury House

Near Tarrant Gunville, north-east of Blandford, stands a fine gate and the remains of what must have been one of the most magnificent houses in the county—Eastbury House. About 1709 Sir George Dodington, a Lord of the Admiralty, bought a farm and lands on which he planned to build. In 1717 he commissioned Sir John Vanbrugh to prepare designs of a house which was to be surpassed in size only by Blenheim and Castle Howard. Twenty years later it was completed at a cost of £140,000. When Sir George died, the house passed to his nephew, George Bubb Dodington, the son of a Weymouth apothecary, who entertained lavishly there and exercised a considerable influence in local affairs.

Eastbury House was a massive building of five great courts and a frontage of nearly 600 feet. The approach was through a great Roman archway. All Vanbrugh's magnificence was displayed there. The Duke of Cumberland, in his memoirs, spoke of a visit to Dodington in 1756, describing the mansion as

> magnificent, massy and stretching out to a great extent in front with an enormous portico of Doric columns ascended by a stately flight of steps: there were turrets and wings that went I know not whither.

The interior reflected

> the taste of the magnificent owner, who had gilt and furnished the apartments with a profusion of finery that kept no terms with simplicity and not always with elegance or harmony of style.

Bubb Dodington had no suitable pictures to decorate the walls, so instead 'he had stuck up immense patches of gilt leather shaped like bugle horns upon hangings of rich crimson velvet'. Some of the carpets, Cumberland suggests, though they were of gold and silver embroidery, betrayed their origins 'from coat, waistcoat and breeches by testimony of buttons, loops and pockets'. Dodington's lack of taste was seen in his town villa, where 'he slept in a bed encanopied with peacock's feathers'.

Dodington, possibly because of his humble origin, had a profound respect for titles and ordered his life at Eastbury to enhance his own magnificence.

> Our splendid host was excelled by no man in doing the honours of his house and table; to the ladies he had all the courtly and profound

devotion of a Spaniard with the ease and gaiety of a Frenchman towards the men. The interior of his mansion was as proud and splendid as the exterior was bold and imposing.

Guests had to come to their host through a suite of apartments to find him 'seated under painted ceilings and gilt entablatures'.

To suit this magnificence, Dodington's clothing was 'rich and flaring'.

> His bulk and corpulency gave full display to the vast expanse and profusion of brocade and embroidery, and this, when set off with an enormous type periwig and deep lace ruffle gave the picture of an ancient courtier in his gala habit.

Every birthday Dodington added to his wardrobe. Perhaps the clothing he had outgrown became the carpets Cumberland noticed. Apparently his guests were mainly entertained, not with cards, but by their host reading aloud from Fielding's *Jonathan Wild*. On one occasion his manners seem to have been at fault, since he was described as lolling in his chair dozing or even snoring at times.

Dodington was to exercise considerable influence in Weymouth affairs. For nearly forty years the two boroughs of Melcombe and Weymouth were 'the property of Bubb Dodington'. The seats 'gave but little trouble'. In 1721 he put in the painter Sir James Thornhill and two Tuckers, one of whom was an East India merchant and manager of Dodington's business affairs. The Tuckers, father and son, were local men and often served as mayors and returning officers, which made votes easily manipulated at elections. Dodington himself was chosen as Member of Parliament for Weymouth in 1734 but preferred to sit for Bridgwater. One of his relatives was returned in 1741. Six years later a new town charter was obtained for which the mayor was instructed

> to address the Right Honourable George Dodington of Eastbury with the thanks of the Incorporation for his patronage of them in their late difficulty and friendship to the whole Community in obtaining by his indefatigable endeavour and at his sole expense the charter and letters patent.

Dodington's own diary gives many details of his handling of the town's affairs. He bargained: 'Mr Tucker and I met Mr Pelham at Mr Scopes by appointment: we settled the Weymouth re-election according to the agreement made on obtaining the new charter'. Dodington's nominee was returned. Another Weymouth member, Francis Dashwood, was a frequent visitor at Eastbury and became a treasurer at the Exchequer. In 1762, almost at the end of his life, Dodington wrote to the Mayor of Weymouth:

> I therefore take the liberty again to recommend my best friend (Sir F. Dashwood) to your favour. Not warmer in inclination though increased in abilities to be the friend and servant of the Corporation and Town of Weymouth and Melcombe. I must confess that the many obligations I have to you all in the repeated marks of your goodness and affection to me on all occasions make me look upon this application as matter of form, not doubting your condescension to my humble request.

A matter of form it truly was, since Dodington controlled Weymouth elections.

> Went to the Duke of Newcastle to give him all the little interest I had towards the electing to a new Parliament. I did it in the County of Dorset as far as they pleased to push it. I engaged also, specially to choose two members for Weymouth which he desired might be a son of the Duke of Devonshire and Mr Ellis of the Admiralty.

Both were returned. This election, Dodington said, cost him £1,580 in buying the four Weymouth and Melcombe seats. This was a trivial sum compared with some of the fortunes spent on purchasing seats in the eighteenth century. Nevertheless, even in a time of fraudulent corruption, the historian of the *Unreformed House of Commons* could describe Weymouth and Melcombe as more notorious than any other borough, and to this corruption Dodington contributed not a little.

Bubb Dodington had no direct heir, and Eastbury House passed to a nephew who offered an annuity of £200 to any gentleman who would keep the mansion in repair. There were no offers. Most of the house was pulled down, the material being sold to cover the cost of demolition. One wing was converted into a smaller dwelling which still stands. At one time the widow of Josiah Wedgwood lived there; later the sporting Squire Farquharson used it for his hunt servants. A century after Corfe Castle's demolition Eastbury's glory departed too.

# Some houses of the great and humble

### Houses of some ordinary folk

Very little of Tudor and Stuart Weymouth and Melcombe Regis now remains, but it is possible to picture the houses of the merchants and their furniture. In Trinity Street, Weymouth, one still stands. It was built by Thomas Giear, merchant, mayor of the town and Member of Parliament. He was a man of some substance but of doubtful honesty, since he and others were found guilty of evasion of customs and heavily fined. His house had a ground and first floor with a projecting porch in the middle and large six-light windows to the rooms. Giear could afford stone fireplaces and a very fine carved oak overmantel which is now in Warmwell House. In the eighteenth century the house was used as Assembly Rooms but has now become a store. Opposite Giear's house in Trinity Street is another early Stuart house which has recently been carefully restored. It is a three-storey building and must, too, have been a merchant's house.

Another merchant family, the Reynolds, lived in St Thomas Street. When Emma Reynolds died in 1583 an inventory was

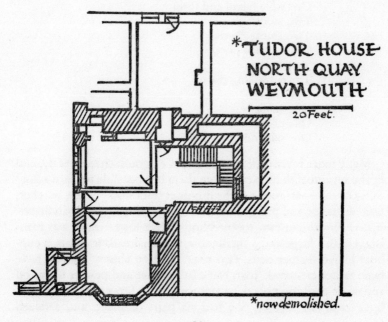

\*TUDOR HOUSE
NORTH QUAY
WEYMOUTH

20 Feet.

\*now demolished.

23

taken, as was usual, of her furniture. This list survives. Her home would appear to have been sparsely furnished, since there were only a settle, a folding table and a round table in the hall, a settle in the parlour, a bedstead and mattress and a chest in the room over the parlour and a cupboard in the room over the hall. Care was taken to list the shelves in the buttery, the closet and the little closet, and to note that the cupboards had locks and keys, as had the back door. Perhaps Emma had given away the rest of her possessions to her children before she died. She might well have possessed, as did another Weymouth resident, the widow Ryves, who died in 1586, a pillow, a red mantle, a feather bed, bolster, sheet, coverlet and blanket, a crock, a candle-stick and two coffers. Joan Ryves had a patched pan and another little pan which she also willed away.

Some years later, in 1617, John Day, a tanner, committed suicide. His goods were seized by the Corporation and consisted of:

|                               | s | d |
|-------------------------------|---|---|
| One bedstead                  | 3 | 6 |
| One mattress of sedge         |   | 4 |
| One coverlet                  | 1 | o |
| One table board and form      | 1 | o |
| Two stools                    |   | 6 |
| Two empty chests              | 1 | 4 |
| Two earthen plates            |   | 2 |
| Two saucers                   |   | 4 |
| Three drinking glasses        |   | 4 |
| One amery                     | 1 | 6 |
| One cradle                    |   | 6 |
| One pillow                    | 1 | o |
| One salt and one glass case   |   | 6 |

Many more inventories survive of Weymouth citizens at the end of the seventeenth century. From them it is possible to learn something of the possessions of the humbler tradesfolk: baker, butcher, weaver, sailor and pulley-maker, widow and spinster. Joan Street, widow, lived in a two-roomed house. Her lower room was furnished with a large and a small table, five chairs, four stools, a cupboard, two feather beds, two rugs and two chests. It must have been rather crowded. Joan had earthenware and pewter to eat off and some cooking pots. Upstairs were stored some chests, trunks, boxes and her clothes. She had six pairs of sheets and a dozen

# THE OLD ROOMS INN
# WEYMOUTH

other linen articles. Her clothes were valued at a pound. To one grand-daughter she left her 'sad coloured petticoat and a green apron', to another four of the best pewter plates, a bed, the best pillow and a little piece of gold. Grace Hardy, another widow, divided her wardrobe in 1693 between two of her kinsmen 'except my sad coloured serge coat and tawny coat' which went to a friend. The tawny coat had apparently been pawned for £1 6s od. One wonders if the executors took the trouble to reclaim it. Another Weymouth lady, this time a spinster living in the High Street, left her broad silk scarf, her under petticoat with the silver lace and her flowered silk petticoat to a cousin. Here was splendour indeed. This lady must have been comfortably off, since she had a Turkey carpet on her floor, with three rugs as well. In addition to the usual two feather beds, linen, stools, chests, chairs and the like, she had three small gold rings and a silver cup, all of which went to a sister.

There are many curious items among these seventeenth-century Weymouth lists of goods and chattels. Why did James Davis, husbandman, own 'an old map and a ship's draft'? Had he been a sailor in his youth? He had also a small Bible and two birdcages and a large variety of cooking implements, including a dripping pan, a basting ladle and a pudding case. Perhaps he had been a ship's cook and had brought home parrots in the cages. Andrew Mathews must have been cooper and sailor by turn. He died possessed of a 'parcel of very bad Newfoundland fish'. Mathews left his land-going clothes, valued at two pounds, to a friend. His sea-going gear was more valuable. At least one Weymouth sailor had made money and could retire to live splendidly; Robert Wall, mariner, had a kitchen, hall and an outer room on the ground floor of his house with three rooms over them. His hall must have been attractive, with its carpet, table, six chairs, and a glass case with books in it. On the walls were two pictures, a looking-glass and two fowling-pieces. Even in his upstairs room he had pictures, a chest of drawers and a ship's lantern; in all, his goods were valued at over £65, of which £15 was in ready money in the house.

In contrast to this splendour was poor William Davey, shoe-maker, whose total goods came to £1 6s od. He had one chair to sit on and a stool for guests, two old bedsteads with bolster and pillow, two earthenware dishes and a solitary fire pan and iron pot. Curiously, he had two chests and a box, but perhaps these were used for storing his customers' shoes; his wardrobe was meagre and seems to have consisted of an old hat and a pair of drawers worth together a shilling. Jonathan Seager, a weaver who lived in St Mary's Street, had even fewer possessions: his old pair of looms was 'good only for firing', and his bed and chest, iron pot, kettle, fire irons and warping bars suggest a bare little home.

When Abraham Adams, a butcher, died, the stock in his shop, beef and mutton, was valued at a pound. In the shop were also his weights, a wooden stock and his tools. Behind were a stable and a field in which were sheep, two small heifers and an old mare, presumably stock for the future. Adams lived next door in a 'new house' of two rooms. The butcher, or his wife, must have liked comfort for there were five cushions. Even more stylish was the home of Richard Bull, a pulley-maker, consisting of hall, parlour, kitchen, cellar and buttery, with a room over the shop and another over the hall. His chairs were upholstered in leather and he had several books. It is a pity we do not know what the pulley-maker read. Indeed, there are many questions which will remain unanswered. Did John Strong, who was a butcher, ever wear the sword, cutlass, belt, leather girdle and bandolier, all worth 12s, or were they inherited from an ancestor? What were the pictures on the parlour walls of the mariner Daniel Wallis? Did he have womenfolk in his family who could play the virginals which were valued at 6s 8d? Were the five 'flower glasses' in his small parlour cabinet bought on one of his trips abroad in the *Two Brothers*, of which he owned a quarter share? When John Murrell, the tailor, died in 1704 he left his house in St Mary's Street 'right against the church' to his wife Mary. He had a shop, kitchen, buttery, stable, hall and study, with four rooms upstairs. No doubt Mary enjoyed the house, but what did she do with the twenty-four glass bottles that her husband left her?

To this tapestry of Dorset folk, castle dwellers, great landlords and town dwellers must be added a sketch of the country yeoman's home. In 1704 Sturton Dawe of East Stoke died in his sixty-fourth year. He had a comfortable hall furnished with a table, four stools, four chairs, two small carpets, three cushions, an old settle and a sideboard. The fireplace had its andirons and racks and there was a warming-pan. The buttery was fully equipped with barrels, a wooden bowl with handles, dishes, a pastry pan, an apple roaster, a porringer, a pestle and mortar, a little brass skimmer and a butter churn. The kitchen had its jack, spits, pans, frying pans, skillets, pot hooks, three little chairs and a pair of bellows. There was also the brewhouse, where not only was beer brewed but cheese was made. Upstairs the main chamber, the hall chamber and the kitchen chamber were fully furnished with feather or flock beds, curtains and bed linen, chests, stools, tables, trunks and a looking-glass. Under 'lumber' were listed sheets, pillowcases, napkins, silver spoons, wearing apparel and a flitch of bacon. Outdoors the yeoman had heifers, a colt, a pig and five stocks of bees, with hay, corn and some agricultural implements. Thus Sturton Dawe was almost self-sufficient in that he made his own bread, butter and cheese, salted his own bacon since he had a special trough for it, brewed his beer and used the honey from his own bees. In all his goods were valued at £62 5s 8d.

Another inventory, that of Jasper Rogers of Cattistock, made in 1710, shows much the same list of possessions, except that Rogers lived in a four-bedroomed house. He, too, ate off pewter but had a mustard pot and a pepper box to adorn his table. He, too, roasted apples before the fire, had his own milk; he had indeed two dozen milk pans. The black marble salt cellar seems rather grand for the milk house. There was a considerable amount of cheese and butter, these valued at £5. The buttery contained cups, jugs, half-hogs-heads and silver dishes. Indoors was stored a quantity of wool. But where Rogers was better off than Dawe was in his livestock; five cows at £16, three horses at £18, 148 sheep at £56, with corn and 17 acres came to a valuation of £132 10s. Rogers had £18 in ready money and a clock stood in the hall, or dining-room as it would be called today. Altogether the impression given by the inventory is of a man of substance living in a comfortable house with all the necessary furnishings of the time.

# CHAPTER TWO

# Dorset prepares for invasion

## The Spanish threat in Elizabeth's reign

Throughout Tudor times men and weapons had to be furnished as part of a county muster of arms. Since no man need journey more than half a day to attend, Dorchester was the muster point for Weymouth and Melcombe Regis. Men of substance were assessed and had to furnish soldiers, weapons and armour. For example, in 1544 the Weymouth bailiffs were called upon to 'send fifteen able footmen, three of whom were to be archers, equipped with a bow and 23 good arrows in a case, sword and dagger'; the rest were to be billmen with bill, sword and dagger. This company was to take part in an invasion of France.

The town owned some armour, since the mayoral accounts note sums spent on cleaning girdles and sword hangers, corslets and daggers. More important, however, from the point of view of defence was the state of the coastal forts and the provision of gunpowder in them. In Henry VIII's reign additional blockhouses were constructed and gunners appointed under fear of a French invasion. A letter from a Weymouth merchant, Henry Russell, to the Privy Council in 1545 described the seacoast as very unprovided for defence. Portland and Weymouth were in great need of powder and there were not enough guns to protect over three miles of easy landing even if earth bulwarks were thrown up for defence. Time and time again, Dorset coastal protection was considered. Guns were sent to Sandsfoot Castle in 1550. Seven years later the Privy Council ordered the Lord Admiral to survey the castles. As the fear of Spain grew, so did the realization that the Dorset coast could afford landing places. The castles were again surveyed in 1576 and lists of ships above a hundred tons drawn up. Three years later it was held that Studland Bay could afford space for forty invading boats, though the tides might be dangerous. Swanage Bay could hold two hundred ships from which men could land at any time. Chapman's Pool, a mere creek, would not be dangerous; Worbarrow would be perilous for an invading force if the wind were in the north-west; given favourable circumstances forty boats might land at Arishmell. Lulworth was not believed to offer landing for more than four or five boats, but a hundred might come in to Bowleaze and Sutton Poyntz. In good weather boats could discharge on the Chesil and at Chideock and Charmouth, and the Cobb at Lyme Regis offered good landing. Musters of men and arms were made; the amount of powder stored in the towns was noted. In 1583 Weymouth had eight pieces of ordnance, four demi culverins, five sacres, two hundredweight of powder, two thousand shot, eight guncarriages with wheels, ladles, sponges and other necessaries, in addition to armour, pikes, arquebuses, swords and a pair of drumheads. Again the justices were called upon to report which parts of the coastal defences needed repair, and a number of eminent men joined an association for the defence of the Queen. Annual musters were held in Dorchester.

There was great fear, however, that the defences were not adequate. Letters were sent to the Council of State in 1586 for obtaining 'some competent and fytte store of ordynance, shotte and powder'. The mayor of Weymouth thought ten or twelve pieces would be needed. Portland Roads were such that 'the Enemys maye there upon the so-dayne arrive and spoile the Towne and Country neare about before any sufficient force of resistance can be assembled'. The twin towns of Weymouth and Melcombe Regis were 'so slenderly provided for that the inhabitants may have to abandon their homes'. The county justices agreed with the Mayor. In the following year news from abroad made it certain that the Armada was 'almost ready to sail'. The Vice-Admiral and the justices spent a March night in Melcombe and thence travelled along the coast to Lyme. The inhabitants were ordered to raise money for half a last of gunpowder with a hundred pounds of match. Other coastal towns were told to do likewise. The muster took place in Dorchester in June, when the Weymouth corslets were to be placed on 'the tallest and meetest persons you have'. The press gangs were at work and contributions were to be raised from various Dorset towns for the fitting out of ships; two ships and a pinnace were to be sent from Weymouth to Howard at Plymouth; all were to be over sixty tons.

In May 1588 Sir John Norris advised that the Dorset forces amounted to 3,000 armed foot and some light horse. This force was to assemble at Weymouth, except for small detachments at Lyme, Bridport and Purbeck. Portland and Sandsfoot castles were to be defended, the one by a hundred foot, the other by fifty. Sir John believed that any considerable separation of these men would be dangerous. If other counties should send in reinforcements, these would be best posted at Abbotsbury and Lulworth. The firing of the beacons on Sutton Poyntz, Ridgeway and Blackdown would be the signal for Sir John himself to rendezvous with his men; the beacon at Badbury would alert Sir Henry Ashley on Badbury Down. Sir John Horsey would come with his men from Cerne, Sir Richard Rogers from Milborne, Mr Trenchard from Ridgeway and Mr Strangeways from Frampton. Beacons at Bubbdown would inform the Somerset forces, Lewesdon Devon and Melbury Wiltshire.

Weymouth fitted up six ships—the *Galleon* of 100 tons with 50 men on board, the *Catherine* and the *Heath Hen* both of 60 tons with 30 men. The *Gold Lion* or the *Royal* of 120 tons with 60 men, the *Sutton* of 70 tons with 40 men and the *Expedition* of 50 tons with 50 men. Lyme sent the *Revenge* of 60 and the *Jacob* of 90 tons.

What part they played in actual events is not known, but certainly an action took place off the Dorset coast. In a flat calm, with Portland Bill abeam, Lord Howard was worried about Weymouth and gave battle, while a smaller engagement developed under the lee of the Bill, when Frobisher in the *Triumph* with five merchantmen, was attacked by four galleasses. Howard thereupon led a line of the Queen's galleons to rescue him. A Spanish prize, the *San Salvador*, was brought into Weymouth. 'Their lordships are credibilie informed that certain chests of treasure and other things of good valewe have been privilie taken out of the Spanish caracke and secretlie deteyned and embeseled . . . they take stricte order to apprehend such persons.' A week later they ordered Sir John Trenchard to send all the brass pieces from the ship to be transferred to Her Majesty's ships with all shot and match. The wine, over fifty pipes of it, was also to be sent by 'an honest master who will have care that there be no waste or spoile'; the rest of the booty might be sold in Weymouth and the money handed to the town.

# Dorset prepares for invasion

According to the inventory, this amounted to sixty-seven empty casks worth 3s 0d each, some beef, beans and vinegar, in all barely £12 in contrast to over £600 worth of ordnance and wine. Since the money to cover the cost of equipping the six ships had not all been raised, surely the town had a very real grievance. Nevertheless, the men of the Dorset coastal towns often dabbled in piracy, so perhaps they reimbursed themselves by other means.

## The threat from the French and Napoleon

At the end of the eighteenth century the country was faced by another threat from abroad. Before it was over every man, woman and child must have heard of the French and have been alive to the danger of war. As soon as England entered on what was to be a prolonged struggle with the French, an Act was passed in 1794 for the raising of volunteers, particularly near the sea coast. This volunteer force was to supplement the militia and to consist of detachments of sixty men with officers; such men would be excused militia service. Subscription lists were opened in Dorchester in July and £2,500 was quickly raised. The idea of raising a force had already been mentioned to Lord Milton, the son of the Earl of Dorchester, in the previous year. He agreed, and at the Dorchester Assizes in March 1794 plans to raise volunteer troops of cavalry were drawn up. The Volunteer Rangers were to wear green jacket and waistcoat, leather breeches, long black boots, a cloak to roll up behind the saddle and a round hat. The enrolment day was to be 3 May and a week later the force met in Dorchester. On 18 June a field day was held at Poundbury, but soon afterwards weekly exercises were suspended during harvest and sheep-shearing. On 5 September the King reviewed three troops of the Rangers at Longbredy Down. By this time the green jacket had acquired yellow buttons with DVR on them, the coat had a small black velvet collar and the round hat a green feather. About 250 paraded on that day, every man with his own saddle and bridle. Unhappily the King would not sign the commissions for Colonel Weld and his son, since they were Catholics. Another review took place a week later, when an ox was roasted. The King again reviewed the troops, this time below Maiden Castle, on the 17th.

The spring exercises began again in April 1795 when the troops paraded at 10 am, each volunteer in his regimental clothing with arms and accoutrements. If a volunteer were not on parade by a

3. Captain Travers in full uniform

4. George III on the Promenade (Gillray cartoon)

5. 'A View of Weymouth Bay' as George would have seen it

quarter past ten he was fined sixpence, if any later a shilling. There seem to have been thirty-seven latecomers. Saturday meetings followed weekly, except when Sherborne fair was being held. Each man seems to have been given three blank cartridges and to have provided good flints. From July onwards carbineers paraded with the Rangers. A church parade was held in October at which sabres and spurs were worn. Parades continued all through the winter. On 17 January there was a funeral parade and the following day a practice was organized with the carbine 'of those motions requisite for light cavalry when mounted or dismounted', noted Captain Travers of the Bridport troop in his diary. It was then decided that swords and uniforms should be left at home, to save them. The meetings in 1796 were usually fortnightly, with a dinner in April. It would appear that some Rangers did not always parade, since half-a-crown was levied as a fine for a first absence with a scale up to a pound for a fourth failure to appear.

One piece of work undertaken by the Volunteer officers was to make returns of all cattle, grain, potatoes, flax and hay in the county, and the number of servants that could be mounted to assist in the driving of cattle. Further details were required of the number of servants that could be furnished with picks and spades. This information was to serve as a basis for the *posse comitatus*, the raising of all men between the ages of fifteen and fifty who were not already engaged in some military capacity. One man, Jesse Taylor of the parish of Tarrant Rawson, a labourer, deserted from the Dorset Militia. An advertisement for his apprehension appeared in the *Dorset and Sherborne Journal*.

The coming and going of regular soldiers, though it had its serious side, considerably enlivened the towns. Recruiting parties passed to and fro. The Light Dragoons went through Dorchester on their way to Weymouth and the inhabitants watched the Volunteers, the Royal North British Dragoons and the Royal Horse Artillery pass through. As at other times, some of the visitors found local wives. Sergeant Allen of the Royal Dragoons married Miss Bennett, the only daughter of a Dorchester hatter; Sergeant Allen was a most eligible young man, as he had recently won a share in a £5,000 prize in the Irish lottery.

Evidently the troops laid themselves out to be agreeable They instructed the local volunteers, who were delighted to witness a display of the Austrian sword exercises, performed with great alertness by Captain Damer's troop; 'their points cuts and parries are such as do honour to themselves and to those that were appointed to instruct them'.

In 1797 Captain Travers noted that his troops fired three rounds in honour of the King's birthday on 28 May and there was a dinner at the Golden Lion, Bridport, paid for out of the absentee fines. Again harvest interrupted exercises. In this year the Rangers changed their name to the Dorset Regiment of Volunteer Yeomanry. Invasion now seemed very possible and secret orders were issued. The sheriff made arrangements for assembling the levies and many thousands of pikes and bills were ordered. It was estimated that nearly 21,000 would be called to arms. An armoury was opened at the new County Hall to receive arms and accoutrements for the militia.

An Act passed in 1798 further stimulated volunteering, and now, in addition to the Dorset Yeomanry, many Dorset towns had their own corps. Between 1798 and 1803 twenty-two companies were raised. The regulations of the Puddletown Volunteer Light Infantry, a force of sixty-two men and nine officers, give a picture of these companies. No man was to absent himself without leave; absentees were to be fined a shilling for a private, two shillings for a drummer, five shillings for an ensign, up to half a guinea for a captain. A doctor's certificate was necessary to cover sickness. To appear on parade improperly dressed meant a fine according to rank. Anyone who spoke or laughed in the ranks after the command to attention was given would forfeit sixpence. Arrangements were made for the collection of these fines. The first beat of a drum was the call to arms and men appearing drunk were to be fined five shillings; non-commissioned officers, on a second such lapse, were to lose their rank. No private was to use his musket for private shooting but was to keep it solely for military purposes and keep it clean.

The Beaminster Town Volunteers, eighty-four strong, were officered by a captain, two lieutenants and an ensign and wore a scarlet uniform with green facings and silver buttons. The Evershot Volunteers had a green silk flag and a small Union Jack; their drum still exists. Of the Weymouth companies, one had a major, a captain, two lieutenants, eleven NCOs, four drummers and a hundred and twenty privates, the other a captain, a lieutenant, an ensign, four drummers and eighty-five privates. In addition, Weymouth raised the Loyal Artillery Company with drums and fifes. After 1803 these scattered volunteer units were organized into three battalions of Dorset Volunteer Infantry, paid as previously at 1s 0d a day of exercise for a private, 3s 5d for an ensign, 4s 4d for a lieutenant, 9s 5d for a captain. In addition to the volunteer cavalry and infantry, companies of fishermen were organized into 'Sea Fencibles'. The reorganization of 1798 did not always go smoothly. The Rector of Symondsbury noted that some of the original volunteers, among them a certain Captain Way, refused to give up their jackets, bearskins and hat stars which had been paid for by county subscription. The Rector calls this 'an unpleasant business'. Meanwhile the constables were busy listing the able-bodied, and the villagers were branding their sheep and cattle. For example, those from Askerswell marked their sheep with an A, their cows and other horned beasts with an A on the right horn, the calves and pigs with an A on the forehoof. Eggardon Hill was the rendezvous for cattle and waggons in case of evacuation. Guides, cattle herdsmen, overseers and pioneers with pickaxes, spades, shovels, bill-hooks and felling axes were to be ready to march, each with 1½ lb of bread. There was a false alarm in the spring of 1798, but it does not appear that the general alert was sounded.

Among the men who answered the call to arms was a Dorset farmer, Henry Kaines, who enlisted in the Yeomanry Cavalry. He had an unfortunate experience on parade in the autumn of 1798 at Cheslebourne. The weather had been wet, but when it cleared Kaines and many others took off their greatcoats and piled them on a cart. 'Mine I never saw afterwards, nor any one there left instead. It was almost new and very large and roomy for rough weather.' As the King was to review the whole regiment at Fordington a week later, it is to be hoped that the weather held.

Dorset men may have flocked to the colours as volunteer soldiers, but they were reluctant to join the Navy. An ugly incident occurred in Weymouth when Captain George Wolfe tried to enlist the help of the Mayor in getting seamen. The Portland quarrymen organized resistance and drove the pressgangs back to their boats. A second attempt to land was greeted by musket fire. Sailors were wounded and Captain Wolfe sustained injury; four civilians were killed in the mêlée. Later a lieutenant and a midshipman on their way to report to the Admiralty were arrested and charged with murder. Captain Wolfe was lodged with them in Dorchester gaol. At the Assizes they were acquitted on the ground that they acted in self-defence. It is possible that many of the coast inhabitants were engaged in wrecking and privateering, which would be more profitable than serving as pressed men.

Peace in 1802 brought a respite to these exercises, but not before there had been consultations as to the cheapest sort of helmet for the Yeomanry, whose old ones had worn out. Colonel Damer was ill with gout, so Colonel Frampton had taken over. The Yeomanry received the thanks of the King and Parliament. They deserved it, for they had drilled carefully. Colonel Frampton had written a manual of instructions which were 'absolutely necessary' with commands for wheeling, doubling, countermarching, diagonal movements and the like.

Renewal of war came in 1803, and with it further instructions if invasion should occur. The Yeomanry changed their uniform from green to blue with red facings, since it was found that the green had worn very badly. Each member of the Regiment was issued with very interesting instructions from Dr Rowley: he advised the wearing of a jersey shirt, flannel waistcoat and drawers next the skin in winter and cotton or calico in summer. At night it was advisable to put on a double cotton or worsted nightcap. Meat, bread and potatoes would preserve muscular strength, but greens and fruit should only be eaten sparingly lest they produced flux. Good malt liquor was advised, with brandy, rum or gin in cold weather, when also, and at night, tobacco was an excellent preservative.

Parade followed parade. In September one corps of volunteers 'dined and spent the afternoon with great hilarity' at Leweston House near Sherborne, the home of their commander. Thence in high spirits, preceded by a band, they marched into Sherborne, joined up with the town soldiers, and proceeded to Lord Digby's park. 'The noble earl received them with great politeness and after he had inspected the ranks they were plentifully regaled from his cellars. They cheered him heartily.' Good malt liquor was obviously enjoyed in the autumn as well as in the winter. The Gillingham volunteers enjoyed an excellent dinner, in their turn, at the Red Lion Inn.

Farmer Kaines was annoyed to find that, though a member of the Yeomanry, he had also been drawn for the militia. He found it very difficult to get a substitute. In the end he found John Cull of

Iwerne willing to serve on consideration of £4 14s 6d, a knot of ribbon and three shillingsworth of beer.

Elizabeth Ham has an amusing comment on her brother Tom's appearance as a volunteer. 'I took pains to teach Tom how to place his hat on his head. Those ugly cocked hats: if they were not well poised they were frightful. These undisciplined youths always wore them bobbing down their backs.' In May 1804 Weymouth was alarmed by the news from Portland that the French were either off the coast or had landed. When Elizabeth heard the news she began to dress. The first person she met was her servant girl with a sweeping-brush in her hand. 'Where are you going?' 'Oh Miss Betsy I am going away, I won't stop a minute longer.' 'Well, put down the brush first; you need not take that with you at all events.' Meanwhile the drums were beating to arms and officers were galloping in all directions. A carriage stood in front of Gloucester Lodge to evacuate the royal family, who were in residence. Fog hung over everything. The Yeomanry began to come into the town. About midday the fog lifted. There was no French fleet off the coast—a large fishing fleet, dimly seen through the mist, may have caused the alarm to be given by the Portland signal station.

There were eight of these signal stations along the coast from Ballard Down to Golden Cap, each with a telegraph apparatus. On the roof of the building was a framework with movable shutters, each painted black with a white spot in the centre. Ropes attached to cranks worked the shutters, and passed through to the room underneath. It was possible to make sixty-three combinations corresponding with various letters and numbers. Each station was manned by an officer and two men, one always on duty with a telescope, scanning the horizon to left and right. It was estimated that the range of vision would be ten or twelve miles. Wind, however, impeded the operations and mistakes were made. At night the beacon watch was maintained at eleven posts.

The arrangements for mobilization and evacuation were amazingly thorough. The whole county was divided into ten divisions. In each were known the number of oxen, cows, young cattle, colts, sheep and pigs, riding and draught horses. Every quarter of wheat, oats, barley, beans, peas, malt, hay, straw and potatoes was listed. The numbers of carts, waggons with four, three or two horses were enumerated. Water and wind mills, sacks of flour that could

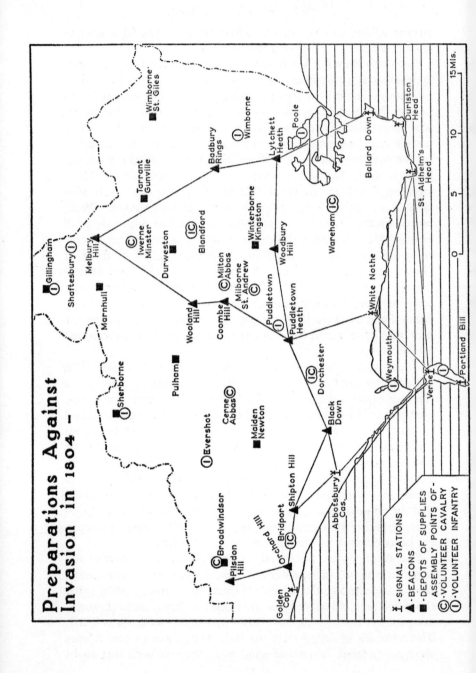

Preparations Against
Invasion in 1804 –

Gillingham
Shaftesbury
Wimborne St. Giles
Marnhull
Tarrant Gunville
Melbury Hill
Sherborne
Iwerne Minster
Badbury Rings
Pulham
Durweston
Wimborne
Woolland Hill
Blandford
Lytchett Heath
Broadwindsor
Evershot
Cerne Abbas
Coombe Hill
Milton Abbas
Milborne St. Andrew
Winterborne Kingston
Poole
Pilsdon Hill
Maiden Newton
Puddletown
Woodbury Hill
Puddletown Heath
Wareham
Ballard Down
Orchard Hill
Bridport
Shipton Hill
Dorchester
Durlston Head
Golden Cap
Black Down
Abbotsbury Cas.
White Nothe
St. Aldhelm's Head
Weymouth
Verne
Portland Bill

SIGNAL STATIONS
BEACONS
DEPOTS OF SUPPLIES
ASSEMBLY POINTS OF-
VOLUNTEER CAVALRY
VOLUNTEER INFANTRY

0    5    10    15 Mls.

be furnished within twenty-four hours, ovens, and the number of 3 lb loaves that could be produced normally and in an emergency were stated. Where there were boats and barges, these were listed. In each division there was a very complete census of inhabitants. It was known how many clergymen, doctors, teachers, constables and tithingmen there were in each division; how many volunteers were actually engaged in military service, how many between seventeen and fifty-five were capable of bearing arms; how many could act as guides either on horseback or foot; how many pioneers, conductors, drivers, overseers, millers, bakers, aliens, Quakers, seamen there were. The number of men and women under seventeen and over fifty-five capable of evacuating themselves or needing help was noted. The detailed arrangements, at least on paper, are impressive. It was laid down that there should be a conductor to every ten waggons and an overseer to every ten drivers. Each division had its place of assembly and its depot. These arrangements surely compare favourably with those of the last war. Such was the census for 1 August 1804. For additional defence there was, of course, the Regular Army; the Hanoverian regiment stationed in Radipole barracks on the outskirts of Weymouth, a brigade of guards, a brigade of militia in temporary encampments on Radipole common; even the Rector of Radipole had to give up his parsonage to the Duke of Cambridge. In Dorchester the Dukes of York and Cumberland had detachments of the Dragoons in barracks. This part of the scheme for the arrangement of the regulars is said to have been drawn up by George III himself, and he certainly reviewed his forces in that year on Came Down.

Among the instructions for the general defence in case of invasion, it was laid down:

> if an enemy should land on our shores every possible exertion should be made to deprive him of the means of subsistence. The navy will cut off his course and the army will confine him on shore in such a way as to make it impossible for him to draw any supplies from the adjacent country. In this situation he will be forced to lay down his arms or give battle on disadvantageous terms.

While those within fifteen miles of the coast were to go to the appointed rendezvous, removing all dead and live stock, horses and draught cattle, a number of 'discreet trusty persons' were to remain in the parishes so long as they were not actually captured by the enemy, to help with supplies for the home forces. It was ordained that the pioneers should be responsible for repairing such roads and bridges 'as will facilitate the movement of our army and render impassable to the enemy'. All these helpers should come with provisions for one day, after which they would draw 1½ lb of bread free every day and if mounted, a ration of forage. They would be paid for all articles taken and a receipt would be given.

In contrast to these solemn precautions was the round of reviews, sham fights and naval fêtes that were arranged to entertain the royal family. The King had a passion for reviews; they were held at Bincombe, at Maiden Castle, on the Weymouth sands—three within a fortnight. Great crowds greeted him with 'God Save the King' wherever he went. He went to sea and also visited Milton Abbey and Stalbridge Park, where he admired the oxen.

At Dorchester a careless dragoon fell asleep with his pipe of tobacco still alight. Fire broke out uncomfortably near the cartridge store in the barracks. In Weymouth, during a grand fête, firework powder was ignited and a servant died; a boy was also run over in the excitement. If there were tension it does not seem to have spoilt the season.

The next year saw the renewal of military exercises; in May 1805 the 1st battalion of the Dorset Volunteers, nearly 700 strong, assembled at Blandford. The weather was unfavourable and prevented exercises. Later in the month General Munro reviewed the troops and on the following day Colonel the Earl of Digby arrived and conferred colours on the regiment, wishing 'the efforts and exertions of the officers and men who compose this patriotic battalion now before me to be ever crowned with victory and success with the blessing of their God who will ever fight for them in a just cause.' Major Cunningham replied, promising to 'protect, defend and preserve the colours untarnished and untainted except by the blood of our enemies or that which may flow from the veins of those heroes who will fly to rally round them in the hour of danger and in the day of battle'. There then followed a long address from the Rector of Ensham complete with quotations from Virgil. A drum-and-fife band played the grenadiers' march, a general salute was paid to the colours, three volleys were fired 'with great exactness' and, after manual and platoon exercises, the parade, headed by General Munro and Lord Digby, marched off in slow time. The colours were deposited in Sherborne Castle.

After 1805 the threat of invasion passed, though the volunteers continued to meet for exercises. They suffered the dramatic loss of Colonel Damer, who collapsed at the Dorchester hustings when voting in the 1807 elections. The Volunteers attended his funeral with black crêpe round their left arms and their sword hilts. A toast to his memory at a dinner was greeted by a dead silence, every person present in tears, 'the only sound that was heard was the bottle passing from one to the other'.

# CHAPTER THREE

## *The visits of George III to Weymouth*

For a brief period at the end of the eighteenth century Weymouth took on the appearance of a fashionable spa. Sea bathing was becoming popular. In 1748 a twenty-one year lease was granted to R. Prouse and J. Bennet to erect two wooden bathing houses on the north side of the harbour. Later, in 1783, it was ordered that a tax of 2s 6d should be levied on every bathing machine. These must surely have been commodious horse-drawn vehicles which may well, as at Lyme Regis, have been carefully drawn up on different parts of the beach with at least fifty yards separating the sexes. At a cost of 1s 6d the machine could, according to a guide-book of the times, be hired with 'umbrella and guide' and also with bathing dresses. These guides might be muscular ladies who actually supported the bathers in their immersions. Sea bathing and indeed sea water mixed with boiled milk and a little cream of tartar were recommended by doctors for various ailments, and it was hoped that George III's health might benefit from a visit to Gloucester Lodge on the Esplanade, where the Duke of Gloucester had passed earlier winters.

Accordingly at seven in the morning of Midsummer Day 1789 the royal party left Windsor in three carriages and, after a leisurely progress through Bagshot, Winchester, Southampton and Lyndhurst, arrived in Weymouth on the last day of June. The King's arrival was announced by guns from a battery facing Gloucester Lodge and from another on Portland. The ships in the harbour were dressed overall and special illuminations and decorations greeted the visitors; according to Fanny Burney half the county of Dorset assembled to welcome their Majesties.

Gloucester Lodge itself was too small to accommodate the party, so the four houses adjoining it were also used. Fanny Burney had to content herself with a very good parlour but with a dull aspect and an attic bedroom. Some of the footmen had to lodge even further away. The royal family and their suite walked out in the evening attended by an immense crowd of sailors, bargemen, mechanics and countrymen shouting 'God Save the King' with stunning effect. Weymouth children loyally sported ribbons round their hats with the same inscription; sailors wore cockades and even the muscular bathing women wore the loyal salutation girdled round their waists; 'flannel dresses tucked up and no shoes or stockings with bandeaux and girdles have a most singular appearance'. The bathing machines bore it in gold letters and on scrolls and devices it adorned every shop and house in the town. Lest the King might not realize what joy his presence was giving, a loyal address was delivered to him on 1 July by the Mayor and burgesses; it dwelt upon the domestic virtues of the royal family. Fanny Burney says that on this occasion the Mayor failed to kneel when taking the Queen's hand. 'Sir, you should have knelt.' 'Sir, I cannot.' 'Everybody does, sir.' 'Sir, I have a wooden leg.'

That day or the next the King took his first bathe 'with great success'. Accompanying the royal bathing machine was a second filled with fiddlers who played 'God Save the King' as His Majesty took his plunge. The princesses also bathed and all took daily walks on the sands and Esplanade. It was to be hoped that the same great crowd did not always surround them with 'volleys of loyal shouts'. Anchored in the bay, facing Gloucester Lodge, were the *Magnificent*, a ship of seventy-four guns, and the frigate *Southampton*, on which several expeditions were made. On one occasion the King listened with interest to the report made by a lieutenant of the watch to the captain. 'It is 12 o'clock.' 'Make it so.' 'You possess, sir,' said George, 'more power than I do. I cannot make it what time I please.' One of the trips by sea was to Lulworth Castle where again the anthem, played by a select band, welcomed the party. 'Mr Weld, the hospitable owner, served a cold collation on a table set with gold plate highly embossed and elegantly engraved with "God Save the King".' Fanny Burney was particularly interested in the Catholic chapel, the altar and the priest's vestments which she saw there, and also one room in the castle where Charles II and James II had slept. Lord Digby was likewise honoured by a visit to Sherborne Castle. These sea trips cannot always have been enjoyable. Elizabeth Ham noted that 'while the King never seemed afraid of the weather the Queen and Princesses always wore dark blue habits on these occasions and I have often seen them look very

miserable and bedraggled on their return'. No doubt they preferred the visits to places of interest in the county that could be
reached by road. On one occasion, when visiting Milton Abbey,
they walked into the house on a green baize carpet over flower-
strewn ground. On another, Dr Ellis tells how the King questioned
a lone woman working in the fields as to where her companions
were, to be told that they had gone to see the King. 'Why did you
not go with them?' 'I would not give a pin to see him, besides the
folk that are gone to town to see him will lose a day's work by it
which is more than I can afford to do for I have five children.'
'Well then, you may tell your companions who are gone to see the
King that the King came to see you.'

Meanwhile, Weymouth enjoyed its season. Every day, Elizabeth
Ham tells us, something was going on to amuse the King, either
a public breakfast, a review or a sail, and a play four evenings a
week with balls on Tuesday and Friday. At the theatre the King
sat in the centre front box. ' 'Tis a pretty little theatre but its
entertainment was quite in the barn style: a mere medley—songs,
dances, imitations and all very bad,' declared Miss Burney. She
was rather less critical of Mrs Siddons's performance as Rosalind.
'She looked beautiful but too large for that shepherd's dress and
her gaiety sits not naturally upon her.' Mrs Siddons's performance
as Mrs Oakley in *The Jealous Wife* she declared a waste of talent;
the Queen apparently disliked tragedy.

On Sunday evenings the royal party honoured the Public
Assembly Rooms with their presence at tea.

> This the King never missed. A cord was stretched from the Ball-
> room to the Tea Room or rather card room where the Royal Family
> took their tea. They were met in the lobby by the Master of Cere-
> monies, Mr Rodber with a candle in each hand, who walked back-
> wards before them up the stairs and into the ballroom, where all
> those who had the entrée were standing within the cord. His Majesty
> was generally dragging the Queen behind him with one hand, bow-
> ing his head slowly and speaking fast to those within the cord, whilst
> she ducked and smiled and spoke according to the time allowed her.
> The Princesses followed according to age and had their say in turn.
> It generally took from three-quarters to an hour to make this short
> transit. The cord was then removed but the door was always left
> open when their Majesties and their invited guests were taking their
> tea.

No wonder, with all this going on, that comparative strangers knocked up slight acquaintances hoping for lodgings and being prepared to sleep three in a bed in order to stay in town.

Public breakfasts were also arranged in marquees pitched in some chosen spot with a platform for dancing, where the public might go to look on, since the King kept one side of the marquee open, and

> His Majesty's loving subjects could enjoy the satisfaction of seeing their beloved Monarch draw a drum-stick through his teeth in which he seemed to delight and to hear his call for 'Buttered Peas' and 'Money Musk' to set the dancers in motion. Country dances were the only ones in vogue but the Princesses never joined in them on these occasions.

The rules for the Tuesday and Friday balls were strict. In 1816 and probably earlier during the King's visit, no gentleman could appear in boots nor ladies in riding habits. Neither ladies nor gentlemen were permitted to dance in coloured gloves. No tea-table could be carried into the card-room. Ladies and gentlemen who danced a country dance could not quit their place till the dance was finished unless they meant to dance no more that night. Swords must be left at the door and no dogs could be admitted.

The King and his family attended Divine Service either at the parish church or on board the man-of-war, where an awning was erected over the quarterdeck. They sat in chairs on the starboard side facing their suite, with the ship's company sitting on forms 'like the pit of a theatre'. 'The attention and solemnity', says Dr Ellis, 'was awful and did much credit to every man on board. The Royal party visited the tars at their dinner and enjoyed the rude mirth of these sons of Neptune.'

In contrast to these events were two rural fêtes, one at Maiden Castle and the other in the fields near Radipole barracks. On the first occasion every regiment stationed in the area had a marquee in which refreshments were served. Among the sports were grinning through a horse collar, jumping in sacks, catching a pig by the tail which had previously been shaved and greased, donkey racing, the last in to be the winner, rolls dipped in treacle hanging on strings to be eaten by boys whose hands were tied behind them. A curious item was a race by women in their undergarments. In 1798, at another rural sports, there was also cheese-rolling downhill, pony races, beer-barrel rolling downhill and cudgelling for a good hat. The prize for grinning was a pound of tobacco. The sack race was rewarded by a leg of mutton and a gallon of porter. Rounds of beef and half-guineas were also awarded. Prudently an umpire was to be chosen 'to settle all circumstances and if he gave satisfaction he will receive half a crown'. The Radipole fields fête appears to have been planned by one of the princesses. All tradesmen who dealt in ornamental wares erected booths on the fields, actors dressed as cooks and riding asses met the royal family and recited the bill of fare which Princess Amelia had composed. There were lotteries and whirligigs and it was arranged that the King should win a penny raffle.

After two and a half months the royal family left Weymouth. Catherine Bowyer wrote to her brother:

We returned late last Night from Weymouth, where we have been spending a delightful fortnight, we were the first Night at a Ball on board the Magnificent one of the pleasantest I ever was at & though the ship had some motion I was not the least sick. We had a very nice supper besides refreshments at the end of every two dances, we did not get to the Inn till after two o'Clock. The next morning we went into Lodgings, very good ones on the Esplanade which the Chapmans had just left. I never saw any place so full as Weymouth was, the King's being there brought a great many fine peoples. The Royal Family sailed in the Southampton almost every day, when the weather was fine. They likewise came to the Rooms every Sunday Night, & drank Tea in the Card Room, where they made their own Party & gave us little people an opportunity of sitting down, Lady Westmorland was in high favour with the Queen & always sat next to her at Tea, which elevated her Ladyship so much, that she would not speak to anything beneath a Countess, though Ld Westmorland made a point of talking to us. We were at three balls, but none of them so pleasant as the Magnificent, though I must say the last was delightful. Mr Bradley (a Lieutenant belonging to the Magnificent & the Gentleman who invited us to the Ball) Dined with us one day, & settled a Sailing scheme for two days after, in their Long Boat. We took Cold Meat with us & dined upon a rock about seven Miles from Weymouth our party was a very large one about fifteen, we walked to an Ale House to drink Tea, then returned to our Rock got on Board where we landed, & rowed home in the Cutter, we had singing almost all the way home, & as soon as we landed at Weymouth a fire Baloon was let off, which had a very pretty effect upon the Waters, after we had amused ourselves with staring at the

Baloon the whole Party walked into our House and went to Supper, though we had a little Music first, in short it was one of the best days I ever spent, though to be sure we had not quite victuals enough, & the Gentlemen wanted more wine, but that was a fault on the right side, as we were going home in a Boat. We did not once go on Board the Southampton, though I danced one Night with Mr Pigot a very pleasant Young Man belonging to it & he invited me, & anybody I chose to bring, but we really had not time. I assure you we enjoyed ourselves the fortnight we were at Weymouth, & went to everything, one Night we took Louisa to the Play, the Royal Family were there & it was a Harliquin entertainment very well executed considering, she was highly delighted, and we were very fortunate in our places.

The Royal Family left Weymouth last Monday, the Magnificent & Southampton sailed that day, the Bay looked dreadfully dull without the Ships, as the Esplanade did, without our Blue Coated friends.

However, Weymouth was to be visited on six or seven more occasions. The doctors were convinced that the King's health had benefited, even though it is not certain that he followed exactly some early nineteenth-century directions for sea bathing:

The most proper time for bathing is early in the morning before which no exercise should be taken; all previous fatigues tending to diminish that force which the fibres when contracted will otherwise have of removing obstructions more effectually; one of the great ends sought for in bathing.

To bathe late in the day (more especially in hot weather) will occasion great depression of the spirits. It is recommended in the morning fasting. Repletion being very improper before going into the sea as it counteracts one of the effects aimed at by sea bathing. Perfect repose of body and serenity of mind are absolutely necessary to promote the purpose of this great remedy. It is impossible to pronounce absolutely with what particular constitutions or temperaments sea bathing will or will not agree; experience only can ascertain when it is or is not proper to each individual respectively. It may be said to agree perfectly, when soon after coming out of the sea, the bathers find their spirits exhilarated and feel a universal glow throughout the system. When the contrary to this happens, it may reasonably be presumed that a further perseverance in bathing may in some degree be prejudical to such persons, and that they should desist at least some time from it.

Certainly when the King returned in September 1791 he was lucky with the weather. Admiral Sir Robert Digby noted in his

journal that when he wanted to bathe after breakfast he was kept
waiting in his machine for an hour by Her Majesty having a working party in a machine in the water. It is a pity that the admiral gave
no further details. It was on this visit that certain officers gave the
King an entertainment at the Victoria Hotel at which a large cake
was provided filled with canaries which flew out when the colonel
cut off the top. On another visit the news of the victory of the Nile
was brought to the King while out riding. He hastened back to
town, since a key was needed to open the dispatch box, and spread
the good news to everyone he met. The troops drawn up on the
sands fired a *feu de joie*.

We are fortunate that several young ladies of the period have
left their journals for us to read, among them Mary Frampton, who
lived at Moreton and was related to the Digbys and by marriage
to the Earl of Ilchester. In 1799 she was considerably embarrassed
when she happened to look out and

actually saw the King and Princess Sophia and their attendants, at
my garden gate. I screamed out, threw down everything about me,
and flew out to them. Mr Damer met me, and told me the Queen and
three other Princesses and their suite were following.

He bid me attend to them, and then kindly went in to Mary and
told what was necessary to be done, helped to put the drawing-room
in order, and bespoke mutton-chops. By this time they all arrived,
and I ran through the house to meet them at the front door. The
King called out, 'Well run, Mrs Frampton'. Into the drawing-room
they went, asked for Mary, talked very easily, and asked for her
cutting-out, which of course they admired. They then proposed
walking, and we all went through my fields to the walks round great
part of the town, and returned the same way, and they seemed much
pleased.

I conducted them into my eating-room, trembling lest the Collation should not be as it ought, but really it was as well prepared as
could be expected on so short a notice—cold partridges, cold meat
of different sorts, and removes of mutton-chops and fruit—tea at
the side-table.

Mary made tea, Mr Damer carried it to them, and I waited on their
Majesties as they ate and Mary on the princesses.

After the repast the female part went into all the bedrooms, and
approved and looked at everything everywhere. In short, they were
all good-humoured and easy. They stayed about two hours, and I
hear from various hands that they were pleased with the day's

48

6. Wolferton House

7. Philip and Joanna. Portraits at Wolferton

8. The room in Trent Manor where Charles lodged

amusement and thought all was so well conducted. This gives us comfort after our bustle.

Five years later Mary wrote:

> Dorsetshire is certainly the gayest county in England—yesterday morning Aunt Frampton took Selina and me in her open carriage to Weymouth, and there we saw the King just before he got upon his horse, and Mr Pitt and a great many other gentlemen with him.

Mary was to meet their Majesties at Lord Poulett's ball, where the King found her a partner with whom she danced four times. Everyone was giving balls—the King, the Yeomanry. There were fireworks for the children and a party where the King spent 'the greatest part of the time playing with all the children, who made such a riot with the Duke of Cambridge. The King stood the whole evening, and carried about the little children and danced with them.'

Nevertheless, there may have been tension during the 1804 visit, since the fear of invasion was very real and a large encampment of troops was at hand for the royal protection. The sea fencibles manned a battery of six eighteen-pounders to defend Portland and Weymouth harbour. Three hundred Weymouth volunteers were on guard to support the Hanoverians quartered in their new barracks in the Dorchester road. Bridport sent in a quota to share in the garrison duty whose 'uniformity of dress, cleanliness of person, martial appearance and steadiness under arms' much impressed the citizens of Dorchester as they marched through the town. By the summer the Duke of Cambridge had arrived to inspect the troops who carried out their manœuvres on the sands opposite the Esplanade. All this must have interested the townsfolk. They might not have been able to share in the celebration dinners but they could perhaps watch the young ladies and gentlemen perform *The Tragedy of Alzira* forming 'a most respectable audience', and knowing that the proceeds were to go to sufferers from a fire in Lyme Regis. By the time the royal family arrived in August the town was 'pretty full'. Soon the *Dorchester and Sherborne Journal* was reporting 'our town was never so gay'. A grand ball at the Royal Hotel, patronized by the royal family, resulted in an uncomfortable crush.

The King followed the pattern of previous visits. He rode out to inspect the troops and took his family on cruises when the Queen, alas, was sea-sick. *The Wife with two Husbands* was performed at the theatre. The greatest crowd ever remembered watched a grand review and sham fight at Bincombe. The bands thundered out the loyal anthem. Hundreds assembled for dinner at the Royal Hotel followed by dancing. The King was so impressed by a sermon that he asked for a copy. At the end of one naval party the fog came down and some of the revellers had to sleep on board. After a review and a most excellent sham fight, this time at Maiden Castle, each private enjoyed a pound of pork, half a pound of mutton, bread and three pints of beer by royal command. During this visit the anniversary of both the King's wedding and his coronation were celebrated with bell-ringing, a public breakfast and a grand fête, somewhat marred by a boy being run over and some rocket sparks igniting fireworks, which caused another death.

The climax of the 1804 season came with a grand naval fête given in the royal yacht in the harbour. To it were invited hundreds of nobility and gentry. The lesser folk must have enjoyed the Dutch fair where trinkets and toys of all sorts were shown. Much mirth, it was reported, was enjoyed. At the theatre *The Wheel of Fortune* and *Of Age Tomorrow* were performed. And all this against the background of the French war.

After Nelson's victory at Trafalgar fears of invasion came to an end and the young ladies could look forward to much naval hospitality.

Oh these naval balls, they were so enjoyable. The measured sweep of the eighteen-oared barge. A coach and six is nothing to it. Then being hoisted on deck enveloped in flags taken from the enemy. Then being safely tucked in the commodious chair to be hoisted on board when timid young ladies used to affect still more timidity.

Princess Charlotte, who was to return for her health on later occasions, when inspecting *Leviathan*, scorned to be hoisted in the chair and actually used the ship's ladder, which suggests that her strength cannot have been in doubt. When not being entertained by the Navy there was the excitement of town balls attended by the officers of whatever militia happened to be stationed at Weymouth. 'The officers of the German Legion', says Elizabeth Ham, 'used to amuse us greatly with their broken English and their vain efforts to try to induce us to try to waltz. This was the first we had ever seen of this kind of dance . . . nothing but country dances were then in vogue.'

Princess Charlotte was in Weymouth for her health in 1814 and 1815. She seems to have bathed in late autumn until severe storms in December brought the bathing season to an end. Evidently she had now grown to enjoy the sea.

My father used constantly to sail with the Princess, and generally also accompanied her on any expeditions—to Portland, Lulworth Cove, Corfe Castle, &c, occasionally, as at the little *hostelries* of the latter places, where the Princess had luncheon, acting as her privy purse.

My mother (who disliked sailing as much as my father enjoyed it) was, however, once or twice prevailed upon to accept the repeated invitations of HRH, when I was included in the party on board the Queen's yacht, *The Royal Charlotte*. I well remember the Princess saying to me 'Are you sick, Harriet?' and in my confusion I answered, whilst making my curtsy, 'No, *thank you*, ma'am', to her great amusement. She wore yellow Hessian boots and the high bonnets then in fashion. We had a capital luncheon in the state cabin—cold meat, &c, of course—as hot luncheons were unknown until at least twenty years after, but the Princess took her repast seated on a sofa on deck with the plate on her lap. When asked what HRH would like to have, she said 'cold beef', and then called out rather loudly, 'with plenty of mustard'.

The Harriet in question was Lady Harriet Frampton.

The Princess's birthday was celebrated with a grand military ball and supper given by the Light Dragoons at Hervey's New Rooms. The townsfolk enjoyed their celebration at Luce's Hotel. A display of fireworks was arranged by those tradesmen who enjoyed royal patronage. Mrs Trelawney Brereton entertained officers of the garrison and 'the fashionable circle who were in residence at this distinguished watering place' at her home in Gloucester Row. It was hoped that a new and more spacious church would soon be built, since there was not one large enough for the now established season that Weymouth was enjoying. The foundation stone of one to seat 900 was laid by the Bishop of Salisbury at the command of Princess Charlotte in the autumn of 1815. The Princess had enjoyed her summer visit, and was gratified to see the letters P C and the Crown in variegated lamps entwined with laurel and the whole embellished with the British Standard, outside the Theatre Royal. At a concert to mark the Prince Regent's birthday, Charlotte performed 'with all condescension possible on the pianoforte where her style was marked with the most refined taste and beautiful expression'. Evidently the princess liked music, though whether she appreciated the military band always in attendance is not reported. She sang Italian duets with a member of the Salisbury choir at a select concert in a voice of 'great compass and elegance'. At the theatre *The School for Scandal* was performed, and *The Irishman in London*. Trips to sea were enjoyed, with visits to Melbury and Cerne.

Princess Charlotte was so sorry to leave Weymouth that she cried when she said goodbye to the Framptons. She had learned as a child to play ducks and drakes there and now had been the centre of a little season. But Weymouth's brief period as a fashionable watering-place was at an end. A lasting memorial to the royal visits had been erected by public subscription in 1810 to mark the King's Jubilee. The King's statue was a demonstration of the town's loyalty and a memorial of its short age of elegance.

# CHAPTER FOUR

## *Some other Dorset visitors, willing and unwilling*

B ecause Dorset was a coastal county, as well as a beautiful one, from time to time people landed on its shores or sought to leave the country from its harbours. Some of them did so in exciting circumstances. Others visited the county in the course of their tours of England; some suffered imprisonment within its castles or merely settled for a time as temporary residents. Medieval kings hunted in Cranborne Chase. Travellers like Leland, Camden, Peter Munday and Defoe have left their impressions. Celia Fiennes rode through it. Wordsworth and Coleridge were visitors by design. Macready the actor retired for a time to Sherborne.

In January 1506 the Archduke Philip and his wife Joanna, Princess of Spain, sailed from Middelburg in the Low Countries with eighty ships for Spain. A storm raged in the Channel and the Archduke and his wife sought safety or were driven on to the Weymouth coast. The townsfolk were alarmed and hastened to send a message to important landowners near by. Sir Thomas Trenchard arrived at the head of some troops, speedily followed by Sir John Carew, both prepared to face what might be an invasion. The uninvited guests were told they could not return on board till King Henry had been informed, and meanwhile they were to be Sir Thomas Trenchard's guests at Wolfeton, near Dorchester. The house, recently completed, was a fitting lodging, with its gatehouse, chapel, long gallery and courtyard wings, only part of which remain. One thing the house did not possess—a man capable of speaking to the royal pair, so a message was sent to one of Sir John's relations, a young cousin, John Russell, living near Swyre, who seems to have been something of a linguist and may even have visited the court at Castile. There is a suggestion that Russell's Spanish proved useful in reporting to Trenchard.

## Some other Dorset visitors, willing and unwilling

When the King heard the news he sent Thomas, Earl of Arundel, with a train of 300 horses to escort Philip and Joanna to Windsor. Arundel arrived at Wolfeton 'in great magnificance and for more state came by torchlight'. Henry's invitation, more properly a command, was accepted and Philip, in a gown of black velvet, a black hood, a black hat and his horse harnessed in black velvet arrived at Windsor. His company, too, of a bare dozen, were in cloaks of sad tawny black. Joanna appears to have travelled separately. Whether young John Russell was in either party is not known, but he certainly appeared at court where royal favour helped him to found the fortune of the house of Bedford. Thus it may have been due to a storm off the Dorset coast that a descendant of Henry Russell, merchant and Weymouth owner of the ship *James*, trading with Gascony and acting as naval transport for ships and mariners during the latter part of the Hundred Years War, was to become one of the great landowners of England.

Weymouth was used to entertaining distinguished guests. When George Trenchard 'being then new knighted' with divers other gentlemen and serving men dined there the meal cost 17s, far less than the breakfast provided in the same year, 1589–90, for Sir Henry Palmer and eighteen men, when the Mayor's accounts show £2 for the meal. One could wish that a record of the food had been made. Viscount Howard, too, received hospitality. For three meals for him in 1602, nine bottles of claret, nine of sack, and six pounds of fine sugar were all bought for the modest sum of 18s. More costly was the 'blankett of sweet meat' given to Lord Waldron and costing a pound. Another interesting item in the Mayor's accounts, given this time to the Town Recorder, who had been very busy arranging affairs for a new Charter, was the present, in recognition of his services, of six pounds of marmalade 'in a fair box' and there pounds of 'conserves of potatoes' at 10s, nine dozen lobsters and two dozen crabs, all at a cost of nearly £9.

Philip and Joanna suffered in 1506 what we would today consider house confinement. A century and a half later Charles II was to experience an alarming time in the county. In September 1651, after the battle of Worcester, he fled south, hoping to sail to France. Disguised as William Jackson, he arrived with some companions at Castle Cary on the 16th. Living at Trent Manor was his friend Colonel Francis Wyndham, married to Anne Gerard. It was decided that Lord Wilmot and two others should ride on to ask for help. Colonel Wyndham was informed that 'a gentleman friend of his desired the favour of him that he would be pleased to step forth and speak with him'. When Wyndham went out to see what this meant he found Wilmot pacing by the stables. The Colonel had believed Charles dead and was delighted to get other news, declaring that for His Majesty's preservation he would value neither life, family, nor fortune. The two men retired indoors to plan for Charles's safe lodging at Trent and decided that only six of the household, Wyndham's mother, his wife, a cousin, Juliana Coningsby, and three servants should know the truth. On the next day Charles arrived to find four rooms set aside for his use. Lady Wyndham gave up her own bedroom since it communicated with a secret chamber between double floors, made, no doubt for Catholic priests harboured earlier by the Gerard family, staunch Catholics, who owned Trent. The King arrived early in the morning, looking haggard but cheerful. The family hurried him indoors where the ladies wept for joy.

Lodged safely at Trent, means were now sought to arrange a passage overseas. Colonel Wyndham set out next day to seek help. Giles Strangeways, to whom he first turned, 'knew not any master of a ship or so much as one mariner whom he could trust'. He sent Charles £100 in gold and suggested that Captain William Ellesdon of Lyme Regis might be approached, since he had helped another royal fugitive. Wyndham accordingly went straight to Lyme where Captain Ellesdon expressed delight at being given this opportunity of showing his loyalty. Enquiries brought the information that one of his tenants, Stephen Limbry of Charmouth, had a coaster about to sail to St Malo. Ellesdon and Wyndham rode straight to Charmouth where an offer of £60 overcame Limbry's very natural fear. Plans were laid for a crossing four nights later. Two rooms were booked for the royal party at the Queen's Arms at Charmouth, where they could lodge till the tide was right. The hostess of the inn was given to believe that she would be helping a young couple to elope from a stern guardian.

Danger, however, threatened at Trent. Excited by a bragging soldier who declared he had killed the King of the Scots, the villagers rang the church bells and lit bonfires for joy. The rumour reached Colonel Wyndham that his house was to be searched, since it was believed that he was harbouring a Royalist. The Colonel admitted that he had a relative staying with him and Wilmot and Wyndham went openly to church to give support to this story.

Next day, 22 September, Juliana Coningsby, the 'eloping maiden' and Charles, as her groom, set out for Charmouth. Wilmot her 'lover' and Colonel Wyndham accompanied them. Captain Ellesdon met them at Monkton Wylde with the news that all was ready and that Charles was now a 'broken merchant' flying from his creditors. Unknown to Charles, he had been recognized, but chivalrous counsel had prevailed and the King was allowed to go on to Charmouth unmolested, where it was hoped they were to embark at midnight.

At ten o'clock that evening Stephen Limbry began to collect his sea chest. His wife, who was evidently conversant with trading routine, asked why her husband proposed to put to sea before he had taken on any cargo. It happened that at a fair that very day Mrs Limbry had heard a proclamation threatening heavy penalties to those who aided the King or any of his party. She told her husband in no uncertain terms that he must not endanger her and his children. The two daughters joined in a violent argument, with threats that the captain of the militia would be told. Feeling that opposition would endanger Charles further, Limbry gave up the attempt to help.

All night the little party waited on the alert at the Queen's Arms, with Wyndham watching on the shore. When the tide had turned it was obvious that no boat would come that night. As he returned sadly to the inn Wyndham saw Limbry, escorted by three women who made conversation impossible. Day had now broken and it was thought wise to depart to Bridport. Wise indeed it was, because suspicions had been aroused.

Wilmot's horse needed shoeing and the smith observed that the three shoes 'were set on in three several counties and one of them in Worcestershire'. The ostler who had brought the horse there had his suspicions further strengthened. The smith immediately went to report to the parish minister who was fortunately at his prayers, thus giving the unsuspecting royal party a respite. By the time the militia was alerted and a warrant for arrest obtained, Charles had left for Bridport. Captain Macey of the militia set out in pursuit.

Here again was danger. As they neared the town they saw that the streets were full of soldiers; Charles had promised to meet

Wilmot there and declared they must 'go immediately into the best inn in the town'. In his own words 'I alighted and taking the horses thought it the best way to go blundering in among them, and lead them through the middle of the soldiers into the stable, which I did, and they were very angry with me for my rudeness'. One can only marvel at Charles's calm, which was almost shattered a few moments later when the ostler, an Exeter man, bringing the horses' oats, declared that he knew the groom's face. Again it was the King's quick rejoinder that he had served as a boy in Exeter, when no doubt the ostler had seen him, that saved the situation.

For over an hour, till a meal could be arranged, Charles had to linger in the yard of the George Inn talking to the soldiers, who were about to sail for Jersey. From the George the party set out again along the London road only an hour before Captain Macey arrived. Finding too many upon the road, they turned north towards Yeovil, thus eluding Macey who rode straight to Dorchester. Luck again favoured the fugitives who, having lost themselves, stopped at Broadwindsor to find out where they were. The landlord of the inn was recognized by Wyndham as a Royalist and was asked to furnish a room, where at the top of the house 'privateness recompensed the meanness of the accommodation, and the pleasantness of the host—a merry fellow—allayed and mitigated the weariness of the guests'. But the peace was shattered by the arrival of forty soldiers whom the constable insisted on billeting there. The night passed noisily, since one of the camp followers gave birth to a child and the soldiers and villagers brawled together while the Poor Law officers hastened to repudiate their responsibility towards the new-born infant.

Next day Charles, Wyndham and Juliana returned to Trent, where the King lodged for the next twelve days. Wilmot meanwhile continued to search for a ship. The days at Trent passed quietly with only one alarm, during which Lady Wyndham insisted that the King should hide in the secret room. Charles appears to have countered his boredom by cooking his own meals and boring holes in coins, which he gave away to the members of the household who 'treasured them up as the chiefest jewels of their family'. On 6 October, again riding with Juliana, Charles left Dorset. On 15 October he sailed from Shoreham in a collier from Poole, the brig *Surprise* under Captain Tattersall.

Later in his life Charles was to return to stay at Crichel House

*Some other Dorset visitors, willing and unwilling*

with his Queen. His memories of the county must have kept him company.

Unlike Philip and Joanna, who were driven by storm to Weymouth, another important visitor arrived deliberately in 1685. On Thursday 11 June the Duke of Monmouth, the illegitimate son of Charles II, landed at Lyme Regis to claim the English throne. He had been a spoilt child and as a young man had honours heaped upon him. As there was no direct heir to the throne, Monmouth's ambitions had grown with the years and now, on the accession of his uncle, James II, he had come to seize what he regarded as his of right. His small fleet of three ships had been nineteen days at sea owing to contrary winds. Landing at the Cobb in the evening of 11 June he knelt on the shore to give thanks to God for preserving 'the friends of liberty and pure religion from the perils of the sea'. Thence with about eighty men he proceeded to the market place, where a blue flag was set up and a proclamation, to be repeated elsewhere, was read. In it Monmouth declared that 'the right of succession to the Crown . . . with the dominions and territories thereunto belonging did legally descend and devolve upon the most illustrious and high-born Prince James, Duke of Monmouth, son and heir apparent'. It further declared that, because Monmouth was absent, the Duke of York 'did first cause the late King to be poisoned and immediately did usurp and invade the Crown'. Monmouth therefore called upon all loyal Protestants to recognize him as King. This announcement was heard by Samuel Dassell, deputy searcher for the customs, who hurried off with the news. Letters were sent immediately by the Mayor of the town to the King and Parliament, to tell them of the landing. For the next three days Monmouth lodged at the George Inn, where recruitment of supporters proceeded. By the end of this time a force of nearly 1,000 foot-soldiers, some say more, and 150 cavalry had assembled, including 80 young men from Lyme itself. Feeling himself now strong enough, Monmouth marched out of the town and took up positions to face the Duke of Albemarle, Lord Lieutenant of Devon, who was coming, it was incorrectly believed, towards them. Men continued to flock to his banner, among them Defoe, until there were more recruits than arms to give them. There was at least one scuffle in which the Mayor of Lyme was shot.

Late on Saturday evening a small force under Lord Grey began a march to Bridport. They believed that they would have to face a much larger force of the King's men in the town. However, on arrival on the outskirts they found no outposts to oppose them and Monmouth's forces entered with only slight resistance. The local levies in the town were completely surprised and it is recorded that the militia horses, frightened by a single volley, ran about riderless. However, firing from the Bull Inn and a stand made by the loyal forces elsewhere in the town checked Lord Grey's advance. The commander, or his horse, took fright; Colonel Venner, another of the rebel commanders, was wounded and retired. The rebels then retreated westward again where they waited in ambush for the attack. After half an hour in which abuse but no shots had been exchanged, the rebels retired along the Lyme road. Nearly back at Lyme, they joined Monmouth again, having failed to capture Bridport. It is hardly surprising that the battle for the town was confused, since the armies, according to Macaulay, were two bands of ploughmen officered by country gentlemen and local barristers. The horses of the cavalry were often plough horses.

At three o'clock next morning the drums beat to arms and Monmouth assembled his army. At ten it marched, possibly 3,000 strong, to Axminster, across the Devon border. On the 18th Monmouth was at Taunton. Three days later Bridgwater was reached with a still growing army. By 6 July Monmouth was a fugitive with his cause lost at Sedgemoor.

But Dorset was to remember Monmouth's rebellion. In September the assizes opened at Dorchester before Judge Jeffreys. His lodgings in the High Street still bear his name. Many arrests had been made. It was felt that if men were absent from their homes about the time of the landing this was sufficient cause for arrest. Macaulay says that the Dorchester court was hung with scarlet trappings to indicate the nature of the reprisals to be exacted. Men of many different Dorset towns were tried. Thirteen from Dorchester were executed; nine from Bridport, five from Wareham, twelve from Sherborne; there was scarcely a town where the bloody heads and quarters were not exhibited. In Lyme the remains of the twelve men executed in the autumn of 1685 hung from the gallows till they fell rotten to the ground. It would appear from the Mayor's accounts of 1686 that he paid a shilling for beer 'for the men that set up the rebels' quarters that were fallen'. In Beaminster men were hanged from the church tower. In Weymouth the gallows stood on what is now Greenhill. The cost here was considerable. On

14 October there was a 'Bill . . . for the Gallows, burning and boiling the rebels executed per order at this Town £15 14 3. Nov 20 paid Mr Mayor . . . for setting up a post with the quarters of the rebels at Weymouth town end 1/6'. Details exist of the disposition of the remains of the twelve men executed. To Upwey were to be sent four quarters and one head; to Sutton Poyntz two quarters and one head, Osmington, Wyke, Preston, Winfrith, Broadmayne, Radipole, Winterborne, Puddletown and Bincombe were all to see what happened to rebels. Within Weymouth there were to be six displays at the Grand Pier, at the town end, near the windmill, at the bridge and at both Weymouth and Melcombe town halls. The list is neatly totalled with its sad sum of forty-eight quarters and twelve heads. In all, over seventy Dorset men perished out of a total of three hundred who were tried. For others transportation was the sentence. Charles Strong of Beaminster sailed for Barbados on a Poole ship named ironically, *The Happy Return*. Richard Hoare and Thomas Bugler of the same town were, with seventy more, put aboard *The Betty* for sale in Jamaica. Simon Poole and ninety more were put aboard in Bristol on the *John*. Poole died at sea. Other rebels were whipped through all the Dorset market towns. Grim though their fate was, for one rebel at least transportation in the end meant prosperity. Azariah Pinney, son of the vicar of Broadwindsor, was transported to the West Indies where in time he built up a prosperous trade. His grandson, John Frederick Pinney, was to return to England a rich man; his descendants still farm in West Dorset.

Two visitors to Dorset, willing ones, came through the agency of the same Pinney family—William Wordworth the poet and his sister Dorothy. They had no permanent home, were very poor and were delighted when their friend Basil Montague introduced Wordsworth to the Pinneys. Montague was tutor at Cambridge to a later Azariah Pinney. An invitation from the elder Pinney brother, John Frederick, went to Wordsworth, apparently inviting him to live rent-free at a family house at Racedown, not far from Crewkerne, a house which stands almost unchanged from that day. In the autumn of 1795 John Frederick sent instructions to his cousin Joseph Gill to prepare for the visitors. 'Inform me,' wrote Pinney, 'whether Betty Darby washed all the linen and cleaned the house properly before the arrival of Mr Wordsworth and acquaint me whether the gardener has weeded all the hedges and put the garden in good order and whether everything looks as it ought—pray examine every part of the hedges in a particular manner and fully describe their appearance.'

An inventory was made of what must have been a pleasantly furnished home. 'Mr Wordsworth has taken a call over of all the things in the house,' Gill was to report—and note was taken of certain cracked plates, a missing wine glass and four broken chairs. One can picture the breakfast-room—'the prettiest little room that can be', wrote Dorothy—with its neat furniture and a large book-case on each side of the marble fireplace. There were comfortable solid chairs, a table, tea chest and reading stand, and elsewhere two mahogany bookcases with 400 books, a leather sofa, a pier-glass in a gilded frame in the best bedroom—'injured' it was noted—a piano, two blue-and-white Delft flower stands and a Delft bottle listed in the inventory but missing. Oilcloth covered some floors, with an Axminster carpet in the best parlour. Even the weights for the kitchen scales were listed, and the tinder-box candle-lighter needed a new steel. The perambulator for measuring distance had a broken handle. This must have been repaired, since Dorothy was to use it on a walk to Crewkerne. The mahogany chair in the maid's room was also broken.

The Wordsworths took possession at the curious hour of midnight on 26 September. They were very short of money, living at that time on £70 a year. There were several occasions when Gill noted that he had lent two shillings for postage or even tenpence. At times the visitors had to live on vegetables. 'I have lately been living upon air and the essence of carrots, cabbages, turnips and other esculent vegetables,' wrote Wordsworth; 'you may perhaps suspect that into cabbages we shall be transported'. Nevertheless the pair were happy. Of Racedown the poet wrote 'it is an excellent house and the country far from unpleasant, but as for society we must manufacture it ourselves'. Dorothy was more enthusiastic. To her friend Mrs Marshall she wrote:

> We found everything at Racedown much more complete with respect to household convenience than I expected. You may judge of this when I tell you that we have not had to lay out 10/- on the house. We were a whole month without a servant, but now we have got one of the nicest girls I ever saw; she suits us exactly and I have all my domestic concerns so arranged that everything goes with the utmost regularity. We walk about two hours every morning. We

have very many pleasant roads about us and what is a great advantage, they are of a sandy soil and almost always dry. We can see the sea if we go 200 yards from the door and at a little distance, have a very extensive view terminated by the sea . . . we have hills—seen from a distance—almost take the character of mountains; some cultivated nearly to their summits, others in a wild state, covered with furze and broom. These delight me most as they remind me of our native wilds.

It would appear that the gardener was not as accommodating as the servant, since he refused flatly to do odd jobs.

The winter solitude, 'winter prospects without doors and within . . . books, solitude and the fireplace', was enlivened by visits. The Pinney men drove over frequently from Bristol and stayed for weeks at a time. They insisted on paying for their board, which must have made them agreeable guests. 'The Pinneys have been with us five weeks, at Christmas and a month since . . . they seem to relish the pleasure of our fireside in the evening and the excursion of the morning. They are very amiable young men, particularly the elder.' Dorothy goes on to comment on his sweet temper and unspoilt character, despite the fact that he had plenty of money. The party went riding, walking, hunting and coursing. The poet 'relaxed the rigour of his philosophic nerves so much as to go coursing', wrote John Pinney, 'and I assure you did not eat the unfortunate hares with less relish because he heard them heave their death groans'. The hares must have helped to enliven the frugal fare. Wood had to be chopped for the fire since coal, very expensive, a small cartful for three or four shillings, had to come from Lyme Regis. The Wordsworths had hoped to welcome Montague also at Christmas, since they were looking after his son Basil, but were disappointed.

The guests did not upset Wordsworth's literary output. They departed in March taking with them a poem, *Guilt and Sorrow*, to give to a Bristol bookseller. William wrote that he was studying Italian and reading French and 'now feel a return of literary appetite, I mean to take a smack of satire by way of sandwich'. Dorothy walked twice to Crewkerne to the post and to shop. She noted that 'the peasants are miserably poor, their cottages are shapeless structures of wood and clay: indeed they are not at all beyond what might be expected in a savage life'. In March Montague paid his promised visit; when he left the poet accompanied him to Bristol for a fortnight's stay. Coleridge was at this time living there and his criticisms were welcomed by Wordsworth. John Pinney wrote on one occasion: 'His *Salisbury Plain* is much altered —I brought it with me to Bristol. It is now at Coleridge's by whom it has been attentively read.' Coleridge visited Racedown, where the two poets read their work to each other. The first thing he read after he came was William's new poem *The Ruined Cottage*. Coleridge then read two acts of his tragedy and next morning William read *The Borderers*. Coleridge, he wrote,

> is a wonderful man, his conversation teems with soul, mirth and spirit. At first I thought him very plain—that is for about three minutes. He is pale and thin, has a wide mouth, thick lips and not very good teeth; longish loose-growing, half curling, rough black hair. But if you hear him speak for five minutes you think no more of them.

Coleridge, too, was charmed by Dorothy, rather more so than John Pinney, who, while speaking of her good humour, declared she did not possess 'that *je ne sais quoi*, so necessary to sweeten the sour draught of human misfortune'. Snow fell; 'Our present life is utterly barren of such events as merit even the short-lived chronicle of an accidental letter. We plant cabbages.'

John Wordsworth, William's brother, sailed in an East India-man; 'my brother saw the fleet sailing in all its glory'. Ten years later, off the very same Dorset coast, John, now in command of the *Abergavenny*, was drowned off Portland. In February 1805 the ship sailed in convoy from Portsmouth with 160 seamen, 159 troops, 51 passengers and 30 Chinese aboard, and a cargo of porce-lain and bullion to the value of £200,000. The ship was driven on to the Shambles. Distress signals brought some help from Portland and some passengers were saved. Captain Wordsworth, it was reported in the *Salisbury and Winchester Journal*, when last seen was clinging to the ropes. 'The mates used every persuasion to entice him to endeavour to save his life; he did not seem desirous to survive the loss of his ship.' His body was later recovered and buried at Wyke Regis and a notice in the same paper in April of a public auction of Riga masts, yards, spars, etc. saved from the *Abergavenny* marked the end of the disaster. But this was in the future and did not mar the happiness of the brother and sister in Dorset. It was not to continue much longer. John Pinney the elder found out that they were living rent-free at Racedown and was angry. He even threatened legal proceedings. The winter of 1796–7 was severe, with heavy frosts and rough snowy weather. The visitors felt the cold and, perhaps more, the threat of legal proceedings. In the summer of 1797, nearly two years after their arrival, they left Dorset to join Coleridge at Nether Stowey.

In 1830 a new royal family came to Dorset, to be lodged in Lulworth Castle. After the July Revolution in France the homeless Bourbon family sailed from Cherbourg to Cowes to seek asylum. Thence they travelled to Poole, where they disembarked for Lulworth, since the wind did not allow of further progress. We get several glimpses of this royal family in Mary Frampton's diary. Her brother visited them at the Castle and noted that Charles X spoke very bad English. He was a tall, thin, gentlemanly man. His brother, the Duke of Angoulême, was 'a very mean looking person'. The young Duke of Bordeaux appeared 'a fine interesting boy with very dignified manners'. Conversation touched on George III's visits to Weymouth and what the country round Lulworth was like. Mr Frampton was surprised that the French king should shake him by the hand. Some days later a return visit was made, with a somewhat amusing prelude. When the Duchess of Angoulême and her lady-in-waiting arrived at Moreton in a gig the butler believed that they had come to see the garden. He left them by the gate while he went to find the gardener. Mary Frampton looked out of the window to observe 'two house-keeper looking persons coming towards the house'. One was dressed in a 'shabby light brown or rather yellowish shawl, cotton stockings, very short petticoats and both wore coarse, weather-beaten straw bonnets'.

Later in the month a more formal visit took place. Harriet Frampton, Mary's niece, describes how, accompanied by her mother and fiancé, they drove over to Lulworth 'and were shown into the great saloon. After a time the door at the end of the room was flung open and "le Roi" was announced'. He came in, accompanied by the Duke and Duchess of Angoulême and the Duke of Bordeaux and his sister. The latter talked to Harriet about her rides on her donkey over the hills. The French party were interested to hear about the English custom of sending pieces of wedding cake to friends, which was unknown to them.

In mid-October the ex-royal family left Lulworth. Peel, the

9. Lulworth Castle. Temporary home of Charles X

10. Macready's home at Sherborne House

Home Secretary, must have been relieved, as he had sent police 'to hover about the Castle', since Charles feared that an attempt might be made to kidnap the Duke of Bordeaux. Mary Frampton says that their departure from the county was regretted; 'they had afforded much historical gossip to the neighbouring families, all but the King having shown themselves everywhere, and, being great walkers, moved about in all directions unlike English people and much to the amusement of all ranks'. One wonders if the police had also to move about. 'The consumption of food during their stay was immense, and one of the reasons whispered for Charles X's departure was that so many dependants lived upon him owing to his residence being remote from any town.' It was said that no food appeared twice on the royal table and it was given away to the poor who complained that the meat was boiled to a poultice and they could not enjoy it. There was also a fear that the King might be arrested for money that he was said to owe from his last stay in England. In the Palace of Holyroodhouse he would be safe from arrest.

Mention must be made of one more temporary resident in the county, but one who stayed for over ten years—the actor Charles Macready. In the summer of 1849 he visited Sherborne from Dorchester, admiring on the way the view of Cerne Abbas and the Blackmore Vale, which he found superb. He explored the town and discovered that Sherborne House was for sale. He called that very day on the auctioneer to enquire the price. Walking in Lord Digby's park next day, he again enjoyed all he saw. 'The stillness of this place, the sleepy quiet reminds me of Thomson's *Castle of Indolence*, not even the coming and going of the sea to make a change—all still, all quiet, but, I think very beautiful. I was delighted with the views in and from the park.' Evidently Macready was in earnest about Sherborne House. Next day he inspected it and learnt that the rent would be £50. The house was 'old fashioned in its adaptation to the needs of a family, but I think it might suit us'. A visit to Lord Digby's steward followed.

In May of the following year Macready came back to Sherborne and signed the lease. Mr Ffooks entertained him to dinner that night. The family then went to Lyme Regis for the summer and took up residence in September. The house might have been old-fashioned, since it was built over a century and a half earlier by one of the Bastard family for Henry Portman. It had a fine stairway

E                                                 65

and painted ceiling of a boar hunt by Sir James Thornhill, one of Dorset's few native painters. The entrance hall was paved with black and white marble. There was a large library in which Macready was to give dramatic entertainments.

The actor entered into the life of the town. He attended a soirée of the Sherborne Literary and Scientific Institution, of which he soon accepted the presidency. He gave much time and thought to helping his fellow townsmen. He opened a night school for poor boys in which he himself taught with other volunteers from among the gentlemen and tradesmen of the town, who attended in turns; he himself was never absent from his post except 'under very urgent necessity'. The school was held in 'an ample and well-lighted room', according to a Government Inspector's report. 'It was attended by upwards of eighty youths, of ages varying from ten to twenty years, but averaging thirteen, and all engaged till evening in laborious employment.' The inspector found the picture of a man lately so famous now giving up several evenings a week to teach the children of Dorset labourers 'the humblest rudiments of that language whose sublimest creatures his genius had for years been accustomed to interpret' an impressive one. Macready would no doubt have been pleased could he have known that, later, Sherborne House would become Lord Digby's Girls' Grammar School.

To his home the actor invited Dickens and Thackeray, among others, to lecture to the Sherborne Institution. Also members of the Mechanics' Institute came to listen to a lecture from Macready on the influence of poetry on the mind; part of his plan to elevate the operative class who on this occasion listened to the actor 'with earnestness of attention that very much interested me'. Sometimes he gave public readings, payment for which went to the Institution funds. In 1861 he left Sherborne, having as a final gesture given a reading of *Othello* and accepted a handsome silver *épergne*. To his evening school boys he gave Bibles, and received in turn a handsome silver paper-knife. Macready had served his adopted town well and it was not surprising that 'all spoke in most affectionate and regretful terms' of his going.

# CHAPTER FIVE

# Three Dorset villages: their trades and occupations

## Puddletown

Sometime in 1724–5 the Vicar of Puddletown, the Reverend Mr Dawney, made a very interesting survey of his village. He had been instituted three years earlier and was perhaps trying to learn something about his parish. He made his record street by street, listing each house with the number of people living in it. In all he listed 156 houses with 605 inhabitants.

There were fewer men, 187, than women, 217, in Puddletown. Of these ninety-eight men were married, twelve widowed and seventy-seven single; there were ninety-seven married women, thirty widows and ninety single women. In addition there were eighty-one boys under twelve years of age, eighty-six girls and four children whose sex was not specified. Thirty more inhabitants were listed as non-parishioners. Some of the Puddletown children, certainly the girls, were away in service, for Mr Dawney frequently made such entries as 'she has three more children out at service'. There were twenty-eight families who themselves employed 'servants or apprentices'; sixteen menservants, nine women, twelve with unspecified sex were noted. The tradesmen who had boys aged between fourteen and twenty-three apprenticed to them included the tailor, shoemaker, barber, wheelwright and woolstapler. Not all the apprentices were local lads. Counting the apprentices and journeymen, forty-two men were actually shopkeepers or craftsmen such as innkeepers, of whom there were five, clocksmith and gunsmith, butcher, baker, weaver, chandler, bricklayer, glazier and painter, plasterer and tiler. Craftsmen allied to agriculture such as miller, wheelwright and thatcher, blacksmith, carpenter and cooper were represented and finally there were the five farmers, six husbandmen, nineteen day labourers and one shepherd. The picture of a self-supporting village emerges. In addition to the farmers and tradesmen were a few professional men, a schoolmaster, the Rev John Chapman 'who boards gentlemen's sons', Henry Skinner 'who teacheth the children to write' and Ann Arnold 'widow, schoolmistress'.

Mr Dawney in his survey made a number of frank comments on his parishioners. There was Sarah Russell 'a poor but idle woman. Her husband has gone abroad and hath left her with three children.' Mary Boyle 'a Quaker, an old maiden, lives by herself' as did Mary Clark, also a maiden who 'entertains lodgers accidentally or people that work in the Town and are strangers'. There were Thomas and Mary Symonds

> two ancient people and Anabaptists with two daughters, Joan aged about 29 and Jane about 22 both of whom I have baptized since I came. They have two sons and two daughters more out at service or married of which I have christened John and Elizabeth who offered themselves for that purpose.

'Mary Savage lives at one end of the house with one son, Arnold, base born in 1712.' 'John Gillet and Agnes with their children Sarah, Agnes and Charles, Agnes born in 1718. It is a question whether John and Agnes were married before they had children.' The vicar sometimes noted the financial circumstances: 'Elizabeth Lovelace born 1659 a maiden, in moderate circumstances', or 'Sarah Whitten, a poor and lame widow'. 'David Danael a widower and John Wellstream widower both maintained by the Parish', and in contrast 'Francis Harris and Mary his wife. Two old and rich people'. From the accounts of the overseers of the poor it seems that Danael received a pound a year house-rent and a monthly allowance of six shillings, later increased to eight. He also had a coat made for him by Reuben Rice, tailor, which cost 2s. His fellow-widower had a lesser allowance of 4s and on one occasion had 4 yards of shirt cloth at 3s 4d given to him. Both men lived in the sixteenth house on the left side of the street near the Green. Rents of cottages on the Green itself were also £1 a year, since Sarah Chillies, a maiden born in 1654, and Sarah Whitten, a poor and lame widow, received this rent for the cottage they shared. The seventy-year-old Sarah got a monthly allowance of 3s and the lame Sarah a shilling more.

There seems to have been a little colony of Anabaptists in

Puddletown, for Mary Wellstream, a widow and Anabaptist living
in New Street, was 'very poor and had three children living at home
and three away in service'. She received 6s a month and sometimes
supplemented this by laying out the dead. In addition to parish
relief, in the year Mr Dawney made his survey at least eleven were
receiving allowances ranging from 2s to 8s a month and the payment of house-rents: there were also a number of illness benefits.
When Hana Genge died in 1723, 2s 8d was paid for her shroud,
7s for the coffin, 2d for altar dues, 1s for watching, and 1s for beer.
'In the second house in Admiston Lane lived Sarah Talbott widow
by herself born in 1655.' When she fell ill Sarah Don was paid 6s
to look after her and a 2s bottle of wine was bought for her. Smallpox struck the occupants of the seventh house in the street near
the Green where lived George Riggs, a day labourer employed by
one of the local farmers, Mary his wife and six children ranging from
one year to sixteen; the two eldest sons were out in service. In
1725 comes the entry 'this family is now broken up by the death of
Father and Mother in the smallpox. Their eldest son John and
William (the seventh child) died of the same distemper.' Help had
been given to the family both with money and nursing. Two of the
children were boarded with Elizabeth Vine, the wife of one of the
village tailors, for five weeks. As her two children both died, and of
smallpox, it looks as if the boarders brought the disease with them.

Mention has already been made of Danael's coat and Wellstream's shirt. The widow Christian Dunman got 4 yards of linsey
and an apron and there are other instances of clothes or material
for them being bought. Sometimes fuel or medicine was also purchased. One of the overseers who cared for the poor when Mr
Dawney was making his survey was Paul Anthony, yeoman, who
lived in a house on the north side of the great bridge beyond the
Mill House, with his wife, four children and a servant 'not of this
parish'. Anthony died in 1746. The inventory with his will shows
the contents of the house.

| Impr. in ye Hall | One round table | 0 | 5 | 0 |
|---|---|---|---|---|
| | One long table | 0 | 2 | 0 |
| | Two oaken chaires | 0 | 2 | 6 |
| | Seven pewter dishes & one stand ditto Wt. 28lbs. at 6d. per pound | 0 | 14 | 0 |
| | Ten plates wt. 9 lbs. at 7d. | 0 | 5 | 3 |

| | | £ | s | d |
|---|---|---|---|---|
| Impr. in ye Hall | Three Kittles Wt. 28 lb. at 7d. | o | 16 | 4 |
| | Two half Hogshds. Iron bound at 5s. | o | 10 | o |
| | One qr. Barrel | o | 1 | 6 |
| | One Brass Boiler. Wt. 11 lbs. at 8d. | o | 7 | 4 |
| | One mash tub | o | 5 | o |
| | One Trendle | o | 1 | o |
| | One Peckax | o | o | 9 |
| In Kitchen | One Furnace | 1 | 7 | 6 |
| | One Round and one long Table Board | o | 3 | o |
| | Three Furms and one Joint Stool | o | 1 | o |
| | Three Chaires and a small stool | o | o | 8 |
| | One pair of Bellows and an Ashes Box | o | o | 6 |
| | A Firepan and Tongs | o | o | 6 |
| | A grid Ire, 2 Iron Candlesticks, 1 Flesh peck | o | 1 | 6 |
| | One spit, one Iron Crock, and one pair of pothooks | o | 1 | 6 |
| In Milk house | One cubbard | o | 1 | o |
| | One earth'n pump 2 cheese vates | o | 1 | o |
| | Five glass Bottles | o | o | 6 |
| | | 5 | 9 | 4 |
| In the Hall Chamber | One Bedstead & Bed Matt. | o | 5 | o |
| | One Rug, one Blank, and one Sheet | o | 2 | o |
| | One Fluck Bolster | o | o | 4 |
| | One Feather Bed and Bolster wt. 67 lbs. at 5d. | 1 | 7 | 11 |
| | Three chairs | o | 1 | o |
| | One Oak'n Chest and 2 Boxes ditto | o | 5 | o |
| In the Kitchen Chamber | One Feather Bed Wt. 62 lbs. at 5d. | 1 | 5 | 10 |
| | One Bolster and Bolster cloth | o | o | 4 |
| | Two Bedsteads one Bed Matt and other lumber | o | 10 | o |
| Out of doors | One Cow | 3 | 10 | o |
| | A stack of Hay | o | 14 | o |
| | One Wheel Barrow | o | 2 | 6 |
| | One Cheese stean | o | 1 | 6 |
| | One stone pigs Trough | o | 1 | 3 |
| | One Rack and Manger | o | 13 | o |
| | For Wearing apparel | o | 15 | o |
| | | 9 | 14 | 8 |
| | brought forward | 5 | 9 | 4 |
| | | 15 | 4 | o |

# Three Dorset villages: their trades and occupations

It is interesting to contrast the contents of Nicholas Gillingham's cottage. He was a labourer who lived at the west end of Ilsington Lane near the heath; his possessions were few.

Inventory of goods & chattels of Nicholas Gillingham late of
Ilsington, Labourer, taken 4 Jan. 1731

| | | | |
|---|---:|---:|---:|
| For his wearing cloths | 0 | 10 | 0 |
| For 2 little old houses that are worth | 8 | 0 | 0 |
| For one bed | 0 | 15 | 0 |
| For two Bedsteads | 0 | 5 | 0 |
| For two potts | 0 | 6 | 0 |
| For two kittles | 0 | 12 | 0 |
| For Pewter | 0 | 7 | 0 |
| For Two Table boards | 0 | 5 | 0 |
| For some Bees some old tubs & Barrells | 0 | 18 | 0 |
| | 11 | 18 | 0 |

The survey of Puddletown made by the vicar may have been kept among the church records, for it passed to his successors. Half a century later another incumbent, Philip Lloyd, added some further details. The population had risen from 605 to 670, with women still exceeding men. Two women appear as shopkeeper and milliner and there is now an apothecary. In other respects the 1769 entries are far less detailed, though it is interesting that the family with the largest number of servants, six, was that of the vicar himself. Since he thus had plenty of help, it was a pity he did not spend more time amplifying the picture of the village which Mr Dawney had painted.

## Corfe Castle

About twenty years after Philip Lloyd had made his additional entries to the Puddletown survey another detailed one, almost as complete as a modern census, was made of Corfe Castle. Again it was compiled street by street, showing the ages, trades and weekly earnings of all the inhabitants. By the end of the century Corfe was nearly double the size of Puddletown, with a total of 1,239 inhabitants; 613 men and boys, 626 women and girls. There were 216 houses listed, giving an average of 5·73 to each house. Some of the homes must have been very overcrowded. In Number 7 High Street lived James Chaffey, the baker, aged thirty-six, Francis his wife, four years younger, one girl of nine, four boys from fourteen to six months and a bachelor lodger, making a total of eight people. Mary Dennis, the midwife, aged seventy, had eight people in Number 15: her son-in-law, Thomas Ridout, the blacksmith, and his son of sixteen, also a blacksmith, another son of eight, and five girls, one of whom, Jane, was Mary Dennis's daughter. One of the children, a twelve-year-old girl, evidently brought in some money by knitting. In the Market Place Joseph Price, breeches-maker, had nine people living with him, including an idiot, aged thirty, on parish relief. The publican and carpenter, who lived next door, had ten in his house. Among the houses where money must have been very short was that of Jane Webber, sixty years old, spinster, in Back Street. She made some money by knitting but was also on parish relief. In the house also lived Thomas Bushrod, a widower of thirty-six, a stonemason dying of consumption and two little daughters of nine and seven. In addition was Hannah Hounsell, a widow whose income from knitting came to 3s 6d a week. She had four daughters whose ages ranged from fourteen to two. Another house had no less than eleven in it. There was Jonas Battrick, a labourer and his wife, with a weekly income of 7s; Robert, a labouring son, and John, a rope-maker's apprentice, both earning 7s, Henry and James, rope-makers' boys, with 3s and 2s, and two daughters of nine and fourteen who both spun flax and earned 3s. The Battrick family was completed by John, a three-year-old bastard grandson. In addition in the house were Thomas Haynes, rope-maker, and Mary his wife, another flax-spinner. The total income for this household came to 46s a week, a not inconsiderable amount for the time.

Among the well-to-do was John Keynton, an elderly surgeon with two servants to look after him. The Reverend John Gent, the curate, lived in High Street with his wife, twenty years his junior, their four children and two young servants. Richard Taylor, the schoolmaster, also lived in High Street; as he took seven boy boarders and had four children of his own, he too had two servants. The parson at this time, the Reverend Sir Thomas Banks l'Ausin, was a middle-aged widower who had, very suitably, a widow to look after him and two servants. The census mentions William Morton Pitt of Encombe, the important man of the district, of independent fortune, Margaret his wife, now aged twenty-four, and their six-year-old daughter. To look after them, and possibly the estate too, were seventeen servants. Even the bailiff at Encombe had two servants. The other important landowner, John Calcraft of Rempstone, employed eight servants to look after himself and his wife.

The prosperity of Corfe had been largely dependent on the Purbeck stone industry, and sixteen stonemasons, one stone-cutter and ten quarriers are mentioned among the men over fifteen years of age; the wages for these trades were among the highest in the village, the cutters and quarriers earning 15s, the masons 9s a week. Another industry was, however, expanding rapidly, that of clay cutting. A flourishing export of clay to the Midlands had recently developed and fifty-five clay-cutters are given in the survey with sixty-four labourers, some of whom may also have been working in the clay pits. Their earnings were usually 10s a week. It obviously did not need much intelligence, since Mathew Hayward, 'amost an idiot', could earn this wage. The third important craft of the village was concerned with flax; the highest-paid workers, of which there were two, earned 16s as dressers and many women supplemented the family budget by spinning. The other craft most frequently mentioned was that of rope- and cord-making. There were six rope-makers and three twine-spinners; the makers had 12s, the spinners 7s, and many children also earned a few shillings as apprentices, or helpers who just turned the wheel. Hutchins describes how this industry was fostered by Mr Pitt

> with the laudable motive of inculcating the spirit of industry among the inhabitants and detaching them from the pursuit of that illicit traffic which from the contiguous situation of this place to the sea coast they had long been accustomed to follow, has established a large and extensive manufactory here for spinning twine, making cordage, dowlas, sacking and sailcloth hitherto at considerable loss and expense to himself, yet undoubtedly of great importance to the community: it constantly employs in its various branches upwards of 200 persons not only in the village but in the neighbourhood.

Whether rope work for men was more profitable than smuggling is doubtful.

The man most nearly connected with the clay trade was William Pike, clay merchant, who lived in Market Place and was at this time a young bachelor of thirty-one. To help him he had a writing clerk slightly older than himself whom he paid 12s a week. Three clay-cutters lived in the house and a woman servant looked after them. The clay industry had been growing since the beginning of the eighteenth century, but the great expansion came with Wedgwood's use of it in the middle of the century. Possibly the order by Queen Charlotte of a tea set of cream-coloured ware with gold and raised flowers upon it stimulated the demand for the 'Queen's ware'. In 1760 William Pike, a Devon merchant, had come to the district and begun development. The clay was cut by hand, stacked in balls for weathering and then loaded into barges on the River Frome, whence it was towed to Poole for transhipment to sea-going vessels for dispatch to the Mersey, thence by pack saddle and later by canal to the Potteries or by sailing barge direct to London. In 1791 Wedgwood entered into a five-year agreement with William Pike for the delivery of 1,200 tons of good clay from the pits which the latter leased from John Calcraft. Pike undertook that Wedgwood should have a monopoly of the clay and agreed to 'use his best endeavour in searching for, discovering and engaging' more clay deposits. It was hoped that pits on Mr John Bond's land at Grange would also be developed. Pike was to get £120 in four equal quarterly payments each year and 1s 6d for each ton over and above the contract amount.

Wedgwood had also used clay from pits in Stoborough leased from Thomas Bartlett of Wareham, and there are articles of agreement between Thomas Hyde of Poole and Josiah Wedgwood for clay at 10s a ton. Hyde in his turn had leased land near Corfe from John Calcraft for twenty-one years. The estimate of the amount of clay shipped to the various merchants and potters from the Purbeck pits varies. Hutchins speaks of 10,000 tons annually, but a more recent estimate by Kenneth Hudson doubles that figure. In 1806 a light iron railway with lengths of line 3 feet long, 3 inches high and 3½ inches wide was laid down from Corfe to Poole harbour. Three times a day, says Stevenson in his Survey of Dorset in 1806, three horses drew a train of ten tons along the line. William Pike was later to amalgamate with Benjamin Frayle, so that there is ample evidence to support the Corfe survey with its emphasis on the growing importance of the Purbeck clay.

The other trades mentioned in the Corfe survey are much like those of Puddletown, and cover the normal needs of a small self-supporting community. The butcher, the baker and the candlestick-maker were there; it is baffling, however, why a community of little over a thousand needed sixteen shoemakers, and ten blacksmiths seems on the large side. The agricultural side of society was represented by eighteen farmers, four shepherds, twelve dairymen, a mole-catcher, eleven carters and a number of labourers. A few fishermen and boatmen are listed, perhaps the part-time smugglers that Morton Pitt hoped to reform. More unusual was a house-painter and a postman.

In times of emergency all boys over fifteen were believed capable of carrying arms, but certainly all children younger than that were held capable of earning. While they might not be employed as young as in the mills of Northern England, the Corfe survey emphasizes that childhood ended early. William Tachell, aged eight, earned 1s 6d turning a rope wheel, and Elizabeth Good-child at eight got 5s 6d for spinning flax. She was better paid or perhaps more capable than Elizabeth Good, aged nine, who only earned 3s 6d. Sarah Keats at ten brought in a shilling from her knitting, Thomas Spencer, a year older, got 1s 6d for labouring. Even boys spun flax. William Spencer at six earned his shilling. Others little more than children helped the barber, the boatmen and the carpenters, as well as working in the stone quarries and clay pits. Of the total of 613 males in Corfe it was estimated that 241 were boys under fifteen. This very high proportion was at-tributed by Hutchins to the fact that many men left the parish and died at a distance and that many women came in and gained settle-ment there. Certainly one schoolmistress's husband was a gardener near London, and the survey says eleven husbands had run away. If the figure of one in seventeen receiving parish relief were true, it would suggest that the Poor Law officers in the parish were rather more easygoing than usual.

Like many other documents, the Corfe survey has several tantalizing entries where further detail would have been welcome. How old were the four old men deemed to be past working age? Why were there only three publicans when Puddletown, far smaller, had five? Were there really enough women besides Elizabeth and Mary Dampier, 'spinsters of independent fortune', to keep the mantua maker fully employed? What did Ann Speech, the dwarf, look like? How old was Mrs Welsh when she eloped? Her husband was seventy-four. Did Ann Dowdle, the wife of a carpenter, when she practised surgery, use any of her husband's tools?

Such then was Corfe at the end of the eighteenth century. Unlike Puddletown, where very few buildings remain from the time of the survey, there are many cottages standing today in the village which must have been among the two hundred surveyed in 1790 or thereabouts.

## Melbury Osmund

In 1801 the first national census was made. There exists in manuscript what may well have been the rough return for this document; it deals with the little village of Melbury Osmund, south of the Somerset border, just off the main Dorchester–Yeovil road.

Melbury had 335 inhabitants living in 65 houses, a lower concentration than Puddletown. Indeed there must have been overcrowding in the house of John Childs, one of the village carpenters, where four adults and ten children were squeezed in. Another carpenter, William Childs, lived with his wife, son and eight daughters. If all the Childs were related—there were nine families so named with a total of sixty all told—the village must have been very closely linked. In Melbury, as elsewhere, the number of females (188) exceeded the males (147).

What is so interesting about this village is that it gives a picture of the domestic system of industry when a cottage craft supplemented farming. There were six farmers and thirty-one labourers, with a gardener, three thatchers and a woodman. Almost without exception the labourers' women were spinners or weavers and eleven men, too, were weavers. The village manufactured dowlas, a coarse linen cloth. In addition, a very strong linen tape was produced to be used in stays. It would appear from the manuscript that the actual manufacturers themselves lived in Melbury; Henry Farr a tape manufacturer, Thomas Cave, a linen man, and William Hodges, a staymaker. In addition to the weavers and spinners were three spoolers, a warper, and a flax comber. The fact that there was so much simple machinery may account for the large number of carpenters, eight in all, in such a small community. Melbury had its miller, baker, shopkeeper and three masons. It had also a rag gatherer and a gatherer of ashes. Since there were few large households, again it is curious that one woman could be employed as a mantle maker. Only the linen merchant, the baker, the parish clergyman, the miller and two farmers kept servants, and these were probably working men in the case of the baker and the miller.

This little community had its 'free school' endowed by Mrs Susanna Strangways Horner. The schoolmaster, Abraham Fisander, got £15 a year with a house and garden. When the Select

*Three Dorset villages: their trades and occupations*

Committee for the Education of the Poor made its survey in 1818 it noted that twenty children attended the school which was sufficient for the needs, not only of Melbury Osmund, but of Melbury Sampford too. In like manner the two villages shared the Reverend William Jenkins. He had come to the village in 1783 to a parish church lately rebuilt by the charitable Mrs Strangways Horner, who gave some beautiful church plate for its use. The family monuments, including one to Mrs Horner's daughter, are to be found in Melbury Sampford Church where, too, Mrs Horner gave a paten stand, a flagon, a silver gilt box and a knife. Thus was the great family of the neighbourhood remembered, though it did not figure in the survey.

# CHAPTER SIX

## *Smuggling*

How far was Hutchins correct when he declared that William Morton Pitt established the rope works at Kingston, near Corfe Castle, to detach the inhabitants 'from the pursuit of that illicit traffic which from the contiguous situation of this place to the sea coast they had long been accustomed to follow'?

Exact evidence about smuggling is not easy to come by, but undoubtedly it was carried on. The calendar of prisoners lodged in Dorchester gaol in the first twenty-one years of the nineteenth century gives sixty-nine men and one woman convicted for this crime. They were imprisoned until they could pay their fines, which ranged from £18 to £340 16s. The average fine was £100, but Job Stokes and James Tothfield had a year's imprisonment because they assaulted and obstructed the excise officers. The Quarter Sessions records for the same period mention four cases. In the summer of 1816 three men, William and Samuel Francis and Edward Lodge, all got six months' hard labour for assaulting the excise officers. Edward Lodge had already in 1812 been fined £340 16s for smuggling and William Francis had been fined £65 5s 5d in December 1815, so it looks as if they were habitual smugglers. In 1817, in the Lent Term, John Groves, too, was sentenced to six months' hard labour for 'making a light on the sea coast of Great Britain for the purpose of giving a signal to persons on board a smuggling vessel'. Three years later William Elliott received three months' hard labour in the Court of King's Bench for smuggling, and in 1821 William Robinson was sentenced to a year for assaulting a customs house officer.

Again and again the same names appear in the gaol calendar. A family living in Swyre was deeply involved. James Northover, a seaman, John, a single labourer and Arthur, another labourer, all appear in the records within six months and Robert Northover, fisherman, turns up two years later. William Waters, aged fifty-four, of Osmington, seaman, was fined £25 in December 1819, while John Waters, aged fifteen, fisherman, was acquitted. Was it because of his age or because he had a 'great impediment in his speech'? Two years later William was fined £100 in February and again in October of the same year. It looks as though he could afford to pay his fine and thought the odds sufficiently profitable to continue. Another Portland family appears several times. George Gibbs, aged fifty, of Portland, fisherman, was sentenced by the Weymouth bailiffs in 1820. In 1821 Thomas Gibbs, aged fifty, and Thomas Gibbs, aged twenty-three, of Portland, fisherman, had six months' imprisonment and had to find securities. Next month Mary Gibbs, of Portland, labourer, was fined £100. There is no absolute proof that these were all of one family, but it is not unreasonable to suppose so. James Gibbs, aged forty, of Kingston, seaman, was ordered by the Mayor of Weymouth to be put aboard His Majesty's ship *The Queen Charlotte* in Portsmouth harbour to be impressed into the Royal Navy. Gibbs did not come from Portland, but the fact that he was sentenced in Weymouth suggests that his activities lay in that quarter.

Where in the county did most of the seventy smugglers come from? By far the greater number convicted in the period came from Weymouth, Portland, Swyre and villages in West Dorset, and of these the greatest number came from Portland itself. Chideock, Bridport, Langton Herring, Portesham, Abbotsbury and Whitchurch Canonicorum all harboured at least one smuggler. Names that are well known today, Comben and Samways, appear in the lists. East Dorset contributed its quota of felons. Worbarrow, Kimmeridge, Langton Matravers and Swanage are mentioned, but not a single Corfe name appears. This may only mean that they were cleverer at escaping capture. A few men came from inland, from Crichel, Bere Regis, Stalbridge, Okeford Fitzpaine. They were probably working along the smuggling routes, which were well defined, to inland towns. Other, strangers, helped the Dorset men, Somerset contributing its quota. Seaton and Beer in Devon, Crewkerne, Southampton and Yarmouth in the Isle of Wight, and even one man from Fishguard all turn up and, most interesting of all, four Frenchmen from Cherbourg appeared before the Mayor of Weymouth. Jacques Deschamp, thirty-six, of Cherbourg, was described as selling fruit. Was he an ancestor of the Breton onion boys? On another occasion Charles Freejoult, twenty-nine, captain of a vessel, Alexander Bosleen, eighteen, seaman, and Frederick Kroloff, thirty-four, seaman, all of the same town, were captured.

The great majority of the convicted smugglers were seamen or fishermen and two were described as sailors. Langton and Portland had quarrymen who smuggled, but almost every trade—labourer, butcher, dairyman, shoemaker, cooper, miller, bricklayer, pig driver—can be found in the gaol lists. Thomas Skinner, servant, 5 ft 4½ in, flaxen hair and blue eyes; William Benbow, slightly shorter, of Shrewsbury, mason, dark with blue eyes; James Channey, blacksmith, of Puncknowle, 5 ft 8 in, dark, 'somewhat yellow', and Thomas Otter of Chickerell, labourer who 'wore earrings', all came before the magistrates. Was George Sims, of More Crichel, exceptional since his trade was given simply as 'smuggler'?

Not all prosecutions seem to have been successful. There are instances of acquittal, and in March 1820 Richard Hooper of Bere, Thomas Westley and Robert Woodgate 'all escaped'; whether from the court or the excise officers is not clear. Generally, however, the fines imposed seem to have been paid in a remarkably short time. For instance, Benjamin White of Wincanton, a servant, dark, swarthy, of orderly behaviour, was fined £8 2s on 24 April 1813. The fine was paid in August. John Mate, of Bere Regis, sentenced in March, paid by July.

That the customs officers had some success in capturing contraband is proved by the advertisements for sale that appeared in local papers. The *Sherborne Journal* carried details of four sales in 1778. In March, at the Customs House at Lyme Regis, there were offered to the highest bidder: 130 gallons of rum, 325 of brandy, 105 of Geneva, 40 lb of coffee berries, 4,509 lb of Bohea tea and 22 lb of green tea. A sale in June at Weymouth included 1,388¼ gallons of brandy and 1,191½ of rum. Within two months 16.536 lb of Bohea tea was offered again at Weymouth, and another sale took place there in December.

Unavoidably there was a well-organized illicit trade from French ports to the West of England. It would appear that French sloops often brought their cargoes, mainly from Roscoff, to Cornwall and Portland; Cherbourg ships came in too, and possibly others from the Channel Islands and Dieppe. H. N. Shore, writing about smugglers in 1892, says of 1833:

11. A ceiling in Sherborne House attributed to Sir James Thornhill

12. A smuggler's receipt

# Smuggling

The following from Cherbourg are in the habit of visiting the English coast chiefly about Weymouth; they range from 27 to 37 tons:

| Betsy | Louise | L'Espoir |
|-------|--------|----------|
| Phoebe }just built | Sisters | Argus |
| Eliza | L'Amité | Bien Aimé |
| | Arthur Eugène | L'Aimable Vertu |

Did the owners choose the name for the last boat listed with sardonic humour? One master, known as French Jack, was said to keep a bottle of cognac in the binnacle to refresh the revenue boat crews when they boarded him. The encounters between revenue men and smugglers were not, however, always so convivial. In 1822 there was a running battle between a revenue cutter and a smuggler in which one of the smugglers was shot and later buried in Wyke Regis churchyard. Riding officers had been organized to keep watch on the trade from early in the seventeenth century; the nineteenth saw the reorganization of the service. In 1829 the coastguard service was given a definite organization with a uniform and the men were armed with muskets. Fast revenue cutters were available with trained crews and ex-Navy officers.

Both the riding masters and the later revenue officers had to face considerable hazards, for the smugglers were ruthless, often armed and frequently well-organized. Philip Taylor, Collector of the Customs at Weymouth, wrote in March 1718:

> The smuggling traders in these parts are grown to such a head that they bidd defiance to all law and government. They come very often in gangs of 60 to 100 men to the shoar in disguise armed with swords, pistols, blunderbusses, carbines and quarter staffs, not only carry off goods they land in defians of the officers but beat, knock down and abuse whoever they meet in their way. So that travelling by night neer the coast and the peace of the country are becoming very precarious if an effectual law be not speedily passed nothing but military force can support the officers in the discharge of their duties.

Lulworth Cove had been a renowned pirate hideout, and now the smugglers were using it. Taylor wrote again in the following year:

> We have Sunday last searched Lulworth Castle belonging to Mr Weld and other suspect houses in East and West Lulworth and seized four gallons of brandy, 12 ells of pepper in the Isle of Purbeck, one anchor of red wine and two anchors of vinegar and knowing it is the constant practice of smugglers to carry their goods off the coast as

soon as possible after landing as Blackmore Vale is the most dis-
affected part of this county abounding in a great number of rogues
... we narrowly searched several houses and seized two anchors of
brandy.

Some years later a Lyme Regis man, Captain Warren Lisle, came
into Weymouth in his cutter *Beehive* with a story that he had seen a
small vessel standing off Portland. The *Beehive* gave chase for
five hours. Eventually some officers boarded the suspected smuggler, were nailed up in the cabin and finally landed at Boulogne.

Two smugglers showed amazing audacity. Thomas Kingsmill
was not a local man, but came from Kent. He and his band operated
along the south coast into Dorset. On 6 October 1747 a band of
thirty, led by Kingsmill, broke into the Custom House at Poole
and loaded their horses with thirty-seven hundredweight of tea.
Openly next morning they rode through Fordingbridge. No wonder this was to be described in court as 'the most unheard-of act
of villany and impudence ever known'. All the gang were heavily
armed. A reward of £500 was offered for their capture. When it was
suspected that one of those who had seen them in Fordingbridge
was about to reveal his information he was brutally murdered,
together with a Southampton customs official. Over a year later
seven of the gang were captured and tried at Chichester for these
murders. Two turned King's evidence and a further trial at the Old
Bailey followed for the attack and for thefts from Poole. Kingsmill was hanged for the crime.

Isaac Gulliver, a Wiltshire man, organized a network of smuggling over several counties. In 1758 four customs officers found at
dawn a large number of casks of spirits and bags of tea on the shore
between Poole and Christchurch, in what is now Canford Cliffs
Chine. One officer went off to get transport for the contraband.
While he was away the other three were assaulted and beaten and
the goods carried off. Twenty pounds was offered for news leading
to the conviction of the smugglers. Such information as came in
was useless. It has been suggested that far too many people helped
the smugglers or benefited from duty-free goods to aid the Customs Commissioners. Old houses on the coast in Portland and
Swanage have been found on demolition to have secret hiding
places in the roofs or walls where contraband could be hidden. A
story is told of a Mr Hooper, Commissioner of Customs, who was
entertaining the Earl of Shaftesbury at his home at Heron Court.

During the meal six or seven waggons heavily laden with casks drove past the dining-room window. Mr Hooper remained seated with his back to the window so that he could truthfully tell a pursuing company of cavalry that he had seen nothing.

Isaac Gulliver seems to have settled about 1768 at Thorney Down in the parish of Handley, north-east of Blandford. It would appear that one of the smugglers' routes from Poole and the coast thereabouts led north through Cranborne Chase to Salisbury. This was wild country, difficult to watch. Gulliver lived at Thorney Down for the next ten years, after which he moved to Kinson, between Poole and Christchurch, a still better place from which to organize the landing of smuggled goods. Meanwhile Thorney Down seems to have been used as a rendezvous and depot. The *Salisbury and Winchester Journal* reported the seizure of tea and liquor near Thorney Down by excisemen in March 1778; they took it back to the supervisor's house in Blandford. That same evening 'a large body of smugglers came with pistols, etc., on horse back, forced their way into the house and carried the whole off in great triumph, shouting along the street, and firing their pistols into the air. While they were loading they gave two casks of liquor to the mob to amuse them.' Small wonder that the offers of rewards for information had little result.

A year later the *Salisbury and Winchester Press* reported on another incident near Thorney Down where 'the excise officer at Cranborne in Dorset having intelligence of upwards of 20 horses, loaded with smuggled goods, passing by that place, he with 6 Dragoons . . . went in pursuit of them and about four o'clock in the afternoon finding the goods in a coppice near Hook's Wood . . . seized them, loaded their horses and began to carry them away'. Forty or fifty smugglers thereupon attacked the dragoons who defended the goods bravely but were overpowered. The smugglers 'beat the soldiers in an unhuman manner, broke their swords, demolished their fire-arms, and carried off their horses in triumph'. Information, this time accurate, led to the apprehension of two of the smugglers who had gone to bed in an inn on the Blandford road.

When Captain Warren Lisle of Lyme Regis retired from the Customs service he came to live at Upwey. From his experience he declared that there were many armed luggers engaged in the smuggling trade operating between Dunkirk and Ostend on one side of

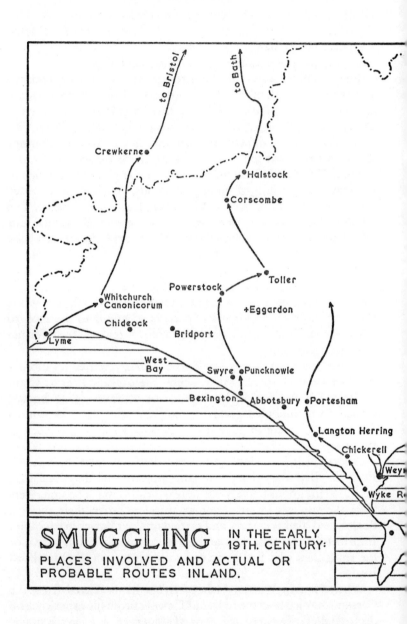

to Bristol

to Bath

Crewkerne

Halstock

Corscombe

Powerstock

Toller

+Eggardon

Whitchurch
Canonicorum

Chideock

Bridport

Lyme

West
Bay

Swyre    Puncknowle

Bexington    Abbotsbury    Portesham

Langton Herring

Chickerell

Wey

Wyke R

SMUGGLING IN THE EARLY
19TH. CENTURY:
PLACES INVOLVED AND ACTUAL OR
PROBABLE ROUTES INLAND.

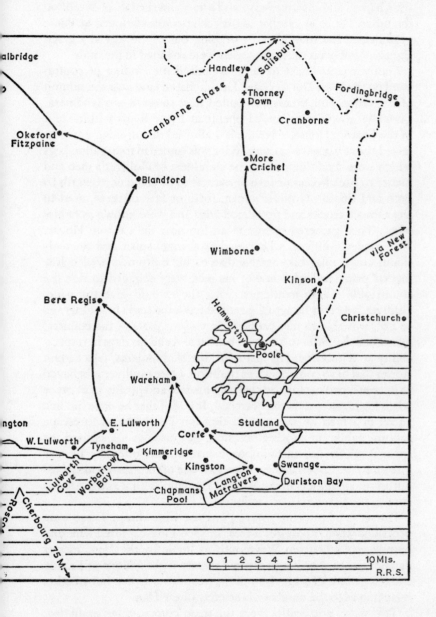

salbridge

Handley

to Salisbury

Fordingbridge

Cranborne Chase

+Thorney
Down

Cranborne

Okeford
Fitzpaine

More
Crichel

Blandford

Wimborne

via New
Forest

Bere Regis

Kinson

Hamworthy

Christchurch

Poole

Wareham

ngton

E. Lulworth

Studland

W. Lulworth

Tyneham

Corfe

Kimmeridge

Kingston

Swanage

Lulworth
Cove

Worbarrow
Bay

Chapmans
Pool

Langton
Matravers

Durlston Bay

Roscff

Cherbourg 75 M.

0 1 2 3 4 5        10 Mls.

R.R.S.

the Channel and the area between Dorset and the Isle of Wight on the other. He believed that the revenue cutter stationed at Poole even helped the smugglers by keeping out of the way at a given signal; possibly up to thirty vessels were engaged in the trade.

Gulliver seems next to have organized the landing of contraband on the West Dorset coast. He purchased land near the summit of Eggardon Hill, where he planted trees to serve as a landmark. Certainly goods were landed openly at Lyme Regis within sight of the Custom House, since the law allowed that nothing could be seized above high-water mark. Wine was landed in four-gallon kegs which were then slung on to the shoulders of Gulliver's men and thence to pack horses or into light carts to be taken northwards to Bath and Bristol. Gulliver's men, forty or fifty of them, used to wear smock frocks and powdered wigs and were known as 'white wigs'. They gathered openly in an inn near the Custom House. No wonder Gulliver, who posed as a wine, spirit and tea merchant, could offer his merchandise to his customers well below market price. Indeed, some of his men were engaged to ride the countryside asking gentlemen what they would give for wine. Gulliver, whether he actually retired from the trade in middle age or not, was able to buy property in various parts of the country, marry one daughter to a Dorset banker and end his days in respectability at Wimborne. His historian, Mr V. J. Adams, tells certain stories that have come down as tradition. Once Gulliver is believed to have escaped capture by chalking his face and posing as a corpse when his house was being searched. It is said that he once hid in a barrel in which he was carried through Poole streets to escape capture, while on another occasion, disguised as a shepherd, he spent a whole day in Wimborne market. Undoubtedly he was known to the Poole custom officers as 'one of the greatest and most notorious smugglers in the West of England', and was reported as such to the London Commissioners.

Dorset gentlemen may have got their wine cheap. There were occasions when others got it free. In 1806 some captured wine and brandy was sent from Weymouth to Poole by the *Dove*, master Samuel Baker. The cargo arrived twenty-eight gallons of brandy and ten gallons of wine short of the quantity shipped. Information is lacking as to the number of the crew of the *Dove*.

Tea, wines and spirits were the main commodities smuggled, but tobacco, silk and wool were also brought in. Mr Florence, riding officer at Poole, on one occasion seized £250 worth of wool loaded in a waggon worth £20 with horses valued at £48. He did not always, however, have things all his own way. Convinced that smuggling was on the increase he asked, in 1806, to be empowered to call on the 14th Regiment of Light Dragoons stationed at Wareham for help since 'the smugglers have got so daring and impudent that they will not give up any quantity of goods except an officer has got a military assistance with him'. A month later Florence was writing again:

> I have been informed that the smugglers have landed a great deal of goods which they kept concealed in caves and sell it out to country people that come for it twice and sometimes thrice a week. About eight or ten of them come together in defiance to any officer. I have applied to the Commanding officer of the 14th Regt. Light Dragoons ... [he] informed me he cannot assist me with a party without orders from the War Office or General.

There is a modern flavour about this situation. Three months later Mr Florence was asked to give details of the occasions when he needed help. The riding officer replied:

> In answer to the Honble. Board's query I must respectfully report that in the instance alluded to I had an information of goods intended to be run in Tyneham parish by a gang of smugglers on horseback, who had made a common practice for some time of carrying goods from Tyneham across the country, but in such large gangs that it was impossible for me to do anything without military assistance. I had never applied for military assistance without having a direct information, or some great probability of making a seizure. And this assertion, I trust, will appear reasonable, when it is considered that the taking out of the military is always attended with an expense, the soldiers expecting to be treated by the officer of Customs.

Poor Mr Florence, tangled up with the War Office, was expected to make captures on his own or to treat the local soldiery out of his own pocket. It is not known if he got help. It must have been more than disheartening for the customs officials and later for the coastguards, since sympathy lay with the smugglers. It is said that the quarrymen on Purbeck would hold the coastguards in conversation to distract them, and build store cupboards in the quarries for the contraband. Tradition has it that goods were stored in the tower of Langton Matravers Church; driven through the main street of Wareham in mourning coaches with the hearse full of live spirits; hidden in the tombs in Kinson churchyard and in the caves along the coast.

In the nineteenth century the smugglers had more refined methods to combat the more efficient coastguard service. The wine might come in concealed in false bottoms. The *Mary Ann* of Poole entered harbour in 1838 with coal as her cargo but with 800 tubs of spirits underneath. More often the casks were strung along a weighted rope and then sunk in shallow water with markers to show the place. They were then retrieved when the time was opportune. A different method was when 'each tub with a bag of ballast attached is suspending by a line from a piece of cork which floats on the surface. The tubs thus arranged are set floating with the flood-tide at the mouth of a river, or creek, and are carried by the current to a point where persons are on the look-out for them'. There is evidence that this method of rafting was used at Poole in 1838. It was probably only the lowering of import duties in the mid-nineteenth century that curbed the Dorset smugglers, since neither riding officers, revenue cutters nor coastguards had managed to do so.

*Various methods of "RAFTING" wine or spirits.*

# CHAPTER SEVEN

# Some Dorset letterbooks

There is probably no more vivid source of history than the letters of the time. Happily business men had to have copies of their correspondence which were usually made into large letterbooks. Three Dorset men, William Willmott, silk thrower, Simon Pretor, grocer and banker, both of Sherborne, and Richard Roberts, linen and rope maker, of Burton Bradstock, have all left some of these books behind. The three men were contemporaries carrying on their businesses at the latter end of the eighteenth century. From the books a picture emerges of the trials, and there were many, of these county merchants.

William Willmott had taken over the control of some silk mills from an uncle, John Sharrer, who had come to Dorset from Whitechapel. Westbury Mill, with a dwelling-house and some land, was leased from Lord Digby. The mill was re-equipped with spinning machines driven by water. Here was trouble to start with. The vagaries of the English climate plagued the manufacturer, who wrote bitterly in 1778 'with the scarcity of water this summer and the expense I have been at on account of a new water wheel . . . has turn'd out the worst summer I ever knew'. Three years later he had to excuse himself: 'my returns are somewhat smaller & will be for 2 or 3 weeks, our stream of water slackens on account of the dryness of the weather again, last week was our usual fair, tomorrow is another . . . the week after is our Races'. The drought continued. 'I never knew such a scarcity in my life almost every spring has been dry'd up round this neighbourhood.' Willmott tried in vain to persuade Lord Digby 'to sink his pond water even $\frac{1}{8}$ of an inch on Thursday of every week just to gain a head of water to serve either me or my people'. Unhappily for Willmott, Lady Digby preferred to see her pond always full. He tried other methods: 'I had resource to the expedient of bribing the person who has care of the water so that this week I hope to go on pretty briskly. Bribery is a fashionable thing but as mine is of the honestest kind, that of self-preservation, I hope it will be deem'd the less pernicious.' Still the weather did not break, so Willmott installed some horse-driven wheels to help out. 'Last Friday being short of water I began the Horse mill and do well.'

In contrast, transport was often affected by weather, 'the excessive hard rains causing several great floods has been of some hindrance to me . . . hardly any silk to go on with'. Since he was dependent on transport for the supply of raw material as well as for dispatching the spun yarn, the state of the roads was all-important. In winter the supply of raw silk was intermittent.

> I am heartily wishing for a favourable account from you [he wrote in January 1773], in respect of trade being a little brisker Xmas being now turn'd and the spring advancing, flatters me with the hope of silk being a little more plentiful . . . hoping you will grant me a further supply as soon as you can conveniently or I believe I must quit Sherborne and take refuge in some other part till Trade Stirs, for having discharged many of my hands which are either starving or are become burdensome to the town, others are incessantly crying for a little work, and cou'd they obtain but a morcel of Barley bread they are happy, very often go days with little or no nourishment, these things move me to be more troublesome to you than I otherwise wou'd be . . . it is enough to melt a heart of stone to hear their complaints.

Trade continued slack, so that in March Willmott described

> the continued cries of the poor people complaining for want of the necessaries of life as well for want of employment is shocking indeed . . . I am in short at a loss how to manage things with them for what little silk I have will not employ a third of them, so that those who have none are jealous of the others that have, the confusion is general and what is worse the Overseers are not so bountiful to the necessitous as I cou'd wish . . . my windsters are ready to devour me.

Two years later, in the winter, he had to dismiss almost a third of his labour force of 150. Yet a few months afterwards he had so much work that he had to refuse orders. 'I worked my mill over hours to make 7 days in a week.'

Sometimes the weather made other difficulties: 'the coldness of the weather and the shortness of days will not permit the hands in general to be so expeditious as at other finer seasons of the year'. In January 1776 'the weather has been so sharp and is still so severe that the people cannot work a great part of the time'. The winter months meant work by candlelight. Dozens of candles were ordered from Bristol; 'the candles are not so good . . . my people make great complaint of their not giving so good & clear a light'. Rushlights were ordered to replace some candles which Willmott intended to return,

> as hardly one in ten will burn little more than half the night many of them gutter out presently—I was in London the week before last and met with some that gave a good steady light and burnt from ten or eleven at night until 7 or 8 in the morning, such as those should be glad you will send me, if not I must burn a lamp rather than use what I have.

It is not surprising that the hands working under such difficulties in winter preferred to go when opportunity arose 'into the Fields a leasing as it is harvest time'. The local fairs and races disorganized work, 'but what with the fairs and having a number of soldiers in a manufacturing town it creates a deal of idleness'. Willmott continued to moan. 'No sooner have we got over one difficulty than another presents itself, for the inclemency of the season is just pass'd over and we just began to get forward a little so this day the whole regiment of the Dorset militia is quarter'd in our Town, and imagine it will be with great difficulty our people can be made to stick to business.' In 1779 over 500 French prisoners were moved through Sherborne to Winchester prison and everyone turned out to see them go through. Poor Willmott—'the hands are so very fickle and fluctuating'. Wearily he wrote, 'I have had a very trying time with my work people'. In this case a local rival was trying to entice them away from Westbury Mill.

The hands were fickle, the weather often inclement and the supply of raw silk to be spun was intermittent. The silk itself presented further difficulties. On one occasion when it was unpacked lumps of salt and lead were found tied up with the hanks. It was often difficult to clean; it sometimes arrived wet, much cut and tumbled; 'it is most of it cut and is intirely full of ends'. This raw silk was cleaned by winding it either by machine or hand on to bobbins. The threads were passed through slots which retained the extraneous material. The clean threads were then twisted or thrown in various thicknesses ready for the weaver. In the process there was bound to be a certain amount of waste, and here again Willmott was full of complaints—the agents were not allowing him a high enough percentage for waste: 'the last Brutias seem to be exceedingly good clean silk, but the waste you have set so low as 5 % which I think can hardly be done'. Like many another manufacturer he declared he could make no profit. To his London suppliers he wrote: 'I have no desire in the least to impose upon you in my prices—I always entertain'd the good opinion of you gentlemen that you would allow the throster a living profit.' So frequently did Willmott complain about the foulness of the silk that he received for spinning, and the inadequacy of the price paid for his work that his correspondents must have learnt to disregard his complaints.

When the silk was spun it was sent, packed in bags, back to London by waggon once or twice a week. It would appear that the carrier was careless. 'Nothing could give me more uneasiness than to have so many complaints about the damaging of the silk in carriage and what makes it more intolerable is having us'd all my endeavours to prevent it.' The thrower told the carrier that he would withdraw his business. He was assured that the Dorset carriers were blameless, it was the London carmen who were at fault, loading heavy parcels on top of the silk. Baskets were tried instead of bags with no better result. Boxes were suggested, to which Willmott replied tartly that this would increase the cost of transport. Sometimes the waggon axles broke or the baskets were left behind at various warehouses.

Damage certainly did occur when a new post-chaise was delivered to Willmott who, in a fine fury, wrote to the carrier:

> I Challeng'd the waggoner by what means he attempt'd to put any person or luggage in a new chaise . . . his answer was to me that you were privy to it and had order'd it . . . now Sir cou'd you immagine I wou'd have bespoke a new chaise of the real value of £34 . . . to be so shamefully us'd in such a manner . . . for the persons who rid in it made all the inside more dirty and spotted it more than ever I shou'd in two years wear, fowls was even put in the seat of the chaise, hampers and some baskets were lash'd on the parts before & tore off paint and wood together, all this, besides both the straps broke in two.

Despite Willmott's frequent grumbles he could afford to live comfortably. He was generous to the London merchants with whom he did business. Regularly at Christmas he sent off poultry by the fast 'machine'. Some turkeys he sent evidently did not travel well. 'I am astonished that the turkeys did not prove good . . . I assure you they were kill'd the very day before they were sent . . . I cannot help thinking they must have been changed somewhere on the road by some ill design & persons.' He apologized that no game was available. 'It is very disagreeable to live upon a spot where a Lord is so very strict over his game.' It is amusing to note that, after a London merchant had made a complaint, Willmott hastened to send off a present with which to mollify him. Poultry, game, cider and beer were all sent, the last by sea from Weymouth. On one occasion, when he was ill, his London agents sent the spinner 'marsh mallow paste' and also medicine. Friends made purchases for him in London. 'Next Fryday for Christening my son Thomas and am now begging you will be kind enough to buy me two or three necessaries which I mean to treat my friends with on that day . . . 4 quarts of real turtle soup if it can be had at Horlans by the Stock Exchange, if not please send some quantity in mock turtle. A fore quarter of the best House Lamb to be had & a Turbot of about 14 or 15 pounds, if can be had, if not a fine cod fish.' It is to be hoped that the fish arrived fresh, considering the hazards of transport. One letter speaks gratefully of a present of some sausages which arrived just before the death of Willmott's mother-in-law 'just in time for her to taste them'. Seeing that she was suffering from severe fits of ague, sausages seem an odd diet. It must have been a disturbed household: 'Mrs Willmott was safely delivered of a fine infant, tho' in some doubt about it staying with us.' Two days later the mother-in-law died 'seemingly without the least emotions of Pain or Anguish. This gives us the greatest hopes that she is now enjoying the heavenly mansions of the Blessed.' Evidently the sausages had not upset her further.

There is much in the letters about the illness of his children. Their deaths are a vivid reminder of the appalling child mortality of the eighteenth century. In December 1773 he wrote: 'Our 3 little ones have been taken very ill since yesterday.' Two months later he was to remark 'it is now six weeks since we lost our little girl Maria Anne'. Smallpox attacked the children. John had been inoculated and was not too ill; Betsy, however, caught whooping cough too and Polly died, 'She having had it all in one with the cough.' Again amid the turmoil Mrs Willmott gave birth to a girl, 'but as we don't know whether she has had the small pox or not you must think fills our minds with anxious thoughts for her well fare and the infants'. His fears were justified. The infant caught smallpox. 'I think we shall lose it.'

This, then, was William Willmott as he showed himself in his letters, a hardworking, somewhat worried silk spinner.

I can never forget the anxious hours, days even years I have experienced in the time, nor the fatiguing days nor the wrestless hours at night in being surrounded and involv'd with a large concern and so small capital to begin with, but hope I shall ever retain the deepest and most grateful thanks for the goodness of Providence which has accompanied me through it and has cast a sunshine on my best endeavour.

When he died of a fever in 1787 his widow continued the business until the son Thomas was old enough to take over the management. Willmott's old Westbury Mill stands today as part of a larger fibre-glass spinning concern, but silk was spun there within living memory.

The second Sherborne merchant who left his letterbook for us to read was Simon Pretor, grocer and later banker. An advertisement in the *Western Gazette* of 1757 speaks of Simon Pretor:

Grocer and Teaman, opposite the Shambles in Sherborne is removing to the Corner of Church Lane, at the Foot of the Shambles, near the Conduit to a House, late in the occupation of Mr John Toogood, mercer, where he intends carrying on the same Business he now does (viz) Grocery, Tea, Haberdashery, Stationary and other goods Wholesale and Retail.

Unfortunately the letterbook which is in existence only begins in 1794 when the grocery business had been long established. By then Pretor seems largely to be leaving the shop to be run by one assistant while another rode the countryside for orders. There were customers in Yeovil, Ryme, Ilchester, Wincanton, Bradford Abbas, Queen Camel, Horsington, Yetminster and Castle Cary.

Pretor stocked a wide variety of goods, as his advertisement announced. He bought his tea in London and stocked eleven varieties, from Bohea at 2s a pound to superfine at 10s. Cocoa came from Frys of Bristol. There is a modern touch in his attempt to increase sales by giving recipes for its making. To Anna Fry he wrote: 'Pray send me a few Printed directions for making your chocolate of which I have some by for which the sale is very dull.' Coffee came from London, Jamaica at 2s, Bourbon at 4s and Turkey at 6s a pound. Sugar and spices were bought both in

London and Bristol; the former included raw, fine, very fine, dry
Barbados, powder, large and small lumps and single and very fine
treble loaves. Mace, nutmeg, ginger, cinnamon and cloves were in
stock. Rice, dried fruit, oranges and lemons, vinegar and oil, salt
and mustard were offered for sale. The range of dried fruit covered
several varieties of raisins, figs, muscatels, almonds, currants and
French plums. There were herrings, anchovies, milk chocolate
and wine. Among other goods were tobacco and snuff, linseed oil,
turpentine and saltpetre, candles, soap, starch, hops, cork, cord
and twine, gunpowder, shot, lead and canary seed. The haberdashery seems limited to gloves, laces, binding in many colours,
and pins.

The London goods were delivered by waggon from Holborn
bridge, or if speed were necessary, by the Royal Clarence coach.
Wine came in direct to Weymouth, where Pretor's own waggon
collected. 'I had a pipe of raisin wine shipped on board some
vessell for Weymouth the 1st March last which I very much want.'
When war broke out he expressed anxiety. 'Pray inform me if the
Weymouth ships sail in convoy. I have mortal spite at these french
fellows.' Goods from Bristol and Exeter also came by road.
Occasionally Pretor bought from a fellow grocer. 'When I was in
Dorchester I think I observed you had some sacks of boiling pease
—if you can spare a few sacks', or 'I have bought best nutmeg of
my neighbour Vowell at 46/–'.

Like Willmott, Pretor suffered from goods damaged in transport.

On Wednesday last in the evening there appeared a Timber carriage in the street opposite Mr Vowells door with the goods on it.
My Hhd [Hogshead] of molasses Trigg'd up (forgive the term if not
in Johnson's dictionary) with a large flint stone as big as a child's
head which having worked a hole *through* the Hhd, molasses com-
monly called Treacle running about the street copiously indeed. My
Hhd sugar with the cleat out and running about the street also: I
had had every reason to conclude from the appearance that the Bulk
of my goods would be found strewed all the way between Waym.
and Sherborne—But how it could be found or gathered together
again appear'd very incomprehensible to me. . . . Your Carter if he
may be so called looked like a Brother Oyster from a Bed of which
I presume he was originally dragged in this world by mistake. However I set all Hands to work and with difficulty before midnight had
got all the Treacle that remained into a fresh cask and the Hhd of

sugar in my Warehouse—which was next day empty'd and carefully weighed in my absence. As I was obliged to go out of Town the next day. On my Return home I was perfectly astonished at being told by my shopman that the Hhd of sugar had lost only 14 lbs and the Hhd of Treacle 14 lb. At least if more were lost it was supplyd by what fell from the clouds.

The carrier has twice arrived from London in the course of the week yet has omitted again to bring my packet of hops.

Many of Pretor's letters were outspoken and written no doubt in anger. He writes in fury to a supplier of lump sugar: 'I was quite shocked at the sight of them. There is not a lump amongst them so good as the worst sample you left here . . . I shall not consider them as my property. And I hereby forbid you sending me any Bastard sugar for I will not have it.' He evidently got a fair reply, for in his next letter he expressed amazement that the wholesaler should talk of going to law. Sometimes the grocer had to eat humble pie. He wrote angrily to the Frys:

Of all the people called Quakers that ever I had the comfort of being acquainted with—I never met with any so very Polite my Worthy friends—I cannot well suppose that both my letters could miscarry . . . I learn that cocoa is advanced. You should have said so. Postage is cheap.

Evidently the reply was such that he had to admit ruefully 'He has completely turned the Balance of Politeness in my disfavour.'

Like all tradesmen, Pretor grumbled about wholesale prices or at least those he had to pay.

The quality of the Tea was but indifferent and you charge me the same Prices as we Sell for here—a blessed Trade methinks—I want some spices but it goes sadly against my will to give 48/- for nut-megs—some other houses advise the best sort at 44/-.

I must observe your Commission and sundry petty changes fall heavy on such fools as myself. For I really believe that those who buy of the Grocers and Tea Dealers in London get more by what they sell than I do.

In common with other traders, Pretor had his difficulties in collecting money owing to him.

Enclosed is your account Balance due to me £30 14 5¾d. This I am sorry to see—and that you should have the immodesty to order another large Parcel of Goods without first settling this acct hurts

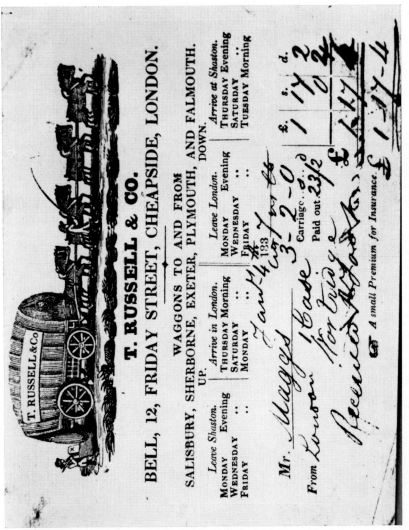

13. The waggoner used by Dorset traders

# WAYMOUTH.

## TERMS

### FOR

# DAY SCHOLARS

### AT

## Mrs. Morris's School,

Where the *French Language*, and all kinds of
*Needle work* are taught.
One GUINEA per *Quarter*.
ENTRANCE 10S 6D.

### FOR

# DAY BOARDERS.

Four GUINEAS per *Quarter*.

## Terms

### OF THE MASTERS

as Per Card of the School.

SCHOOL opens after the present *Vacation* Jan. 19.

J. LOVE Printer, Waymouth, 1790.

14. Notice of terms at Mrs Morris's school

me much—And I here hereby inform you that no more goods will be sent you from this Shop without money paid for it—And the above balance materially and very considerably lessened.

To the Rev Mr Beaver, who had protested, Pretor wrote on 27 January:

> I must confess I am quite concerned to observe by your letter that my sending your Bill to the End of the year should give offence. It was sent for the special purpose of guarding against mistakes—and as my time the last year so much occupied otherwise that I was unable to be so much at my shop as I could wish—I was there every day from Christmas to the end of the past week settling and balancing my accounts I therefore caused every Acct to be drawn out to the End of the year: and I have not a conception that any Gentleman would be offended at my endeavouring to be regular to prevent mistakes.

Simon Pretor sold his business shortly afterwards. He was over seventy and in indifferent health, being crippled with lumbago. He had a large family, some of whom were a real responsibility. He was more interested in his little estate and in his banking, but he meant to get in the money still owing to the grocery. 'As I have long left my trade and you have often been applyed for for payment, I have now to inform you that if the amount is not forth with paid I will take legal methods to compel it.' And even more tersely: 'If I don't see or hear from you about it you may take the consequences.' In May 1796, a year after the sale of the business, he told the Rev Mr Whalley that he proposed to charge interest on fifteen months; 'my clerk shall call upon you for that purpose'.

Richard Roberts, of Grove House Mill, Burton Bradstock, the third of our letter-writers, had more in common with Willmott than Pretor, since he was a manufacturer. His letterbooks cover the period from 1807 to 1815—rather later than the others—and deal with his spinning and weaving business. He produced a large variety of linen, coarse canvas and wrapping materials, sailcloth, sheeting, tarpaulin, towelling and several kinds of twine and thread. Part of his mill still stands by the River Brit, near the church in the village.

Roberts came of a Welsh family, his grandfather settling in Chilcombe. Richard married Mary Hoskins, a widow and owner of Grove House. When the letterbooks open Roberts had been in business for eight or nine years and was flourishing, since he planned a considerable expansion in 1811 with the introduction of new methods. Burton Bradstock was in the flax-growing part of Dorset, so that Roberts's chief interest was in linens. His letters are full of enquiries about flax prices and the amounts that could be bought, and also about the supply of hemp for coarser materials. This was difficult, as war interrupted the trade with the Baltic countries. Nevertheless, Roberts was anxious to use the latest methods of preparing and dressing flax. Stevenson, compiling his survey of Dorset at the time, believed him 'to be the first man to apply machinery in this part of the county to breaking, swingling and spinning flax into thread'. Roberts ordered Mr Lee's patent machinery for dressing flax and hemp without water, and indeed acted as an agent for it in the county.

By 1814 Roberts could write: 'I have now three watermills all in the parish of Burton two for spinning flax, tow and hemp which are constantly at work. Flax is grown in abundance around and also hemp of a very good quality. I have some new and excellent machinery just set going.' And later: 'I have two of the best mechanics in the spinning of flax and two now with me from Leeds that are fitting up and making new machinery for me on the best and newest principles. We have this year in the neighbourhood one of the best crops of flax I have seen for many years.'

Roberts employed over 100 hands, many of them children from neighbouring workhouses. He writes to the poor law overseers of Shepton Mallet: 'I am in want of more [children] than my parish can supply. 10 to 16 or 18 years: if you have any 10–12 girls mostly I will take them free of expense except a suit of working clothes and a suit for Sunday of the better sort.' Roberts promises 'that they will be taken proper care of by people appointed for the purpose and fed with good and sufficient victuals and not worked more than 12 hours a day. They will be sent to church every Sunday and taught to read and say their catechism.' He preferred girls as apprentices; when they were as old as thirteen or fourteen he would only take them on trial lest they should not 'conform to such rules and orders as are laid down, which is sometimes the case when they are so old'. He found the eight-year-olds generally better workers to train as spinners as they were 'most obedient to command'. These children would be apprenticed to the trade. Roberts was also wanting children as non-apprentice servants. There are other letters addressed to Cranborne, Ottery St Mary and even to

Westminster overseers seeking parish children. There is no mention of the rate of pay, but it would probably be from 1s 9d to 2s a week, which was the rate in the ropeworks at Bridport. Roberts paid his adult weavers 10s to 14s a week. He found difficulty in getting enough skilled labour. 'As to a good flax dresser it is hard to find such a person as can be recommended. There are some that have been brought up in this business in my shop . . . many of this sort of workmen are of a loose or bad character.' Certainly Roberts was to find this true of one of his employees who, after six years, stole his ledger and cash book and 'by rubbing and erasing and adding much made out £166'. This man, Thomas Roberts by name, tried to make out that he was a partner in the firm and set about collecting the accounts for himself. 'I can't', said the mill-owner, 'at present get no lawyer or magistrate that knows what to do.' In despair a letter was circulated repudiating the man as an uncertified bankrupt and thief. In the same year another unpleasant incident occurred. Samuel Hoare, who had been employed as a carpenter, was sent north to Castle Cary to learn how to set up flax and tow machinery. He was subsequently dismissed or left, taking some of the hands with him. He then, one day, got back to the mill and made drawings of the machinery which he sold and also made parts for others—a piece of 'daring impudence'. After prosecution had been threatened an apology was published in the local papers. Roberts's concern was large enough after the expansion to employ two carpenters and a blacksmith. He was prepared to pay fifty guineas a year with a house or rooms for full-time work or 15s to 18s for four days' work a week. One young blacksmith so employed, 24 years old, 5 ft 8 in tall, with sandy hair, had been a member of the Falmouth militia and asked for a transfer to the Dorsetshire local force.

In 1812 Roberts was prepared to take on another pupil.

With me you will be able to learn in any branches of the linen manufacturing more than any other person in this country can show you because mine is a general manufactury of sail cloth, ducks, sheeting, table linen, napkins plain and figured, wrappings, and packing cloths upon the newest and best principles. All bleaching, etc. and my terms will be 100 guineas for your learning with the advantage of what work you may do whilst learning. . . . You would learn the mode of bookkeeping also. You will have to live with my foreman close by the works in a neat house and small family, either to board with them or by yourself ... come on trial for four or six weeks.

The 'neat house' may have been built by the mill owner; he wrote frequently about wood prices and often bought clean deal for making machinery and for cottage houses. He also bought raw iron and copper for the same purpose.

Roberts's two letterbooks show that his trade was quite extensive. His foreman toured all the south coast ports getting orders, and there are letters addressed to places from Penzance in the west, Fishguard and the Channel Islands, to Langport and Portsea in the east. In addition there is much correspondence with traders of the inland towns about deliveries of huckaback towels, tablecloths and children's diapers. Sometimes there was difficulty with the colouring. 'The napkins and towels I am sorry to say are neither blue striped owing to the blue yarn not being of a fast colour and entirely came out in the bleaching.' The manufacturer sold material suitable for women's aprons and common smock frocks for men and boys. At times Roberts grew flax himself or acted as agent for others. He traded in this way with Belfast. He would have 'nothing to do with chemical processes. I steep, wash in a mill, boil and lay out on the grass, the bleaching articles used are pot and pearl ash.' He seems to have done work for other Dorset manufacturers; there are many letters to Cox & Hine of Beaminster, and to Hounsell & Co of Bridport, for example.

From his letters Roberts gives the impression of being quick to seek new openings for his mills. He got a contract from the Navy Board for bags for ships' biscuits and began to explore the possibility of supplying bread bags too. He made enquiries about mailbag canvas, about cloth that was used in the mines, about hoppacking and hammock-making, though here he found his men very shy and averse to have anything to do with it'. He had just lost his foreman who had left him abruptly, which added to his troubles. He, too, found his hands fickle and complained that they went off fishing. And then there was an apprentice who ran away. 'I shall not advertise him as a run away apprentice,' he wrote to the mother, 'I would not want to hurt your feelings.' Roberts also supplied twine and shoemaker's thread in fine and superfine four-ounce or two-ounce balls and wick yarn made from tow for lamps. Some of his goods he sent by waggon to the ports and thence by sea. The cloth was sent wrapped in bags, for which he charged.

Like his fellow traders, he had trouble in getting money owing to him. One of the men with whom he dealt at Totnes went bankrupt; forged bank notes came his way and, though he tried not to allow credit, he had to write for one settlement. 'I am sorry you again put me to the unpleasant task of writing to you . . . if it be not sent immediately you will not hear again from me but through another channel which will be very unpleasant.' To another: 'I am quite astonished at the excuses you are making for non-payment of the bills . . . you have no right to ask me for the least further indulgence after so many excuses.' He could write tartly to a client: 'I am astonished as I had a right to expect you would not have so unguardedly written what is perfectly false and in a manner so repugnant to the common modest civility in dealing with any man.' But Roberts was quite capable of behaving in this way himself.

One November night in 1814 the family of five had to jump naked out of their chamber windows to prevent themselves being burnt to death. There had been baking that evening, the bread coming out of the oven at midnight. About four o'clock in the morning one of the servants heard the sound of fire which had spread from the oven to a pile of faggots standing near by or to some linen cloth hanging up in the room. The property was insured for £300 with the West of England Fire & Life Insurance Company and the account of the incident, duly certified by the parish minister and churchwardens as to its accuracy, was immediately dispatched.

For some years Roberts had been in indifferent health. He had asthma, for which he asked if a vapour bath would help. He was much afflicted with a complaint in his stomach and bowels. It was not surprising, therefore, that he encouraged one of his sons, still a very young man, gradually to take over part of the management. Rheumatism made him ill, and there was all the trouble connected with the death and burial of his brother, who had died abroad. Promotion had to be arranged for his son Francis, serving in the Navy. Possible anxiety and overwork lay at the root of his ill-health. He wrote miserably to a Swindon apothecary to whom he had been recommended: 'I am now about 60, have lived a regular and steady life . . . my digestion seems bad, I am often languid and full at my stomach. My stomach is of a dropsical nature when my legs swell up.' Roberts did not die until six years after he sought this help from Swindon. He had, however, thought about his tomb. In 1812 he declared that he wanted 'a good tomb of Portland stone'.

Here and there in Roberts's letters are glimpses of the citizen and the family man. He writes to the Clerk of the County in 1811: 'What is to be done about the beacons, as soon as it is known there is no watch they will all fall a prey to the lawless. If I may give them away or sell them . . . the hut is made of clods and furze with a small door.' Apparently Roberts had to pay ninepence a year rent to the farmer on whose land the beacon stood. He undertook a great deal of personal trading; there are enquiries in the Channel Islands for butter, ham, cattle and wheat. He was in touch with the Weymouth customs officer about duty on French brandy. Some of the purchases were for others. He buys 6 cwt of Irish bacon, cheese and butter, sugar, fruit and wines 'for myself and friends'. To his agent in London: 'I beg you to buy a barrel of good white herrings as cheap as you can . . . for the poor of our parish. Provisions are very dear for the poor.' This was in 1812 when bread reached famine prices. No wonder he could say ironically 'the times are excellent for farmers'. Nevertheless Roberts, despite his ill-health, could boast that he had always at least a month's work in hand for his mill. While he lived the Burton mills kept going. His sons did not possess his energy. The spinning trade went first. Competition from larger concerns for imported fibres necessitated more capital than was available, so the mills came to an end. Willmott's silk mill stands as part of a living concern, Pretor's bank buildings, now the National Provincial, can be seen in Sherborne, but of Richard Roberts's mills part is a storehouse for machinery, part is in ruins, though Grove House itself still stands.

# CHAPTER EIGHT

# Crime and Punishment

The problem of crime and punishment is not a recent one. How to accommodate prisoners and what to do with them deeply concerned the Dorset magistrates towards the end of the eighteenth century. The county gaol was 'in a ruinous and insecure state', so orders were given for it to be rebuilt at a cost of £4,000. This prison stood at the foot of High East Street in Dorchester. Thomas Howard, the prison reformer, visited the new prison in 1787, where he found 32 prisoners, men and women. Howard condemned the new gaol as being 'built on a bad place, a better one, proposed by Mr Pitt having been overruled'. Almost as soon as the rebuilding was completed it was found to be too small and new plans were discussed for yet another building. At the March Assizes in 1787 fifteen justices, among them William Morton Pitt, declared 'that the gaol in its present state is insufficient and requires an enlargement of its site'. Extensions to the new gaol were considered; plans were sent to Morton Pitt, who consulted a London architect, William Blackburn. The latter had already designed several gaols in co-operation with Howard, embodying the latest ideas on penal institutions. Howard is reported to have said that 'Blackburn was the only man capable of delineating upon paper his idea of what a prison should be'. The architect reported unfavourably upon the proposed extension, since it made no provision for separate confinement for the different types of prisoner, apart from sex; he said that apartments were inadequate in number, since two to a cell furthered the possibility of escapes and would also have a bad effect on morals, as it made impossible 'the principles of solitude and separation from whence the hope of reformation springs'. Moreover the building was damp and unwholesome, the cells were not properly ventilated, the outside courtyards were too small, the walls were insecure and built of bad material and the health of the prisoners was endangered.

Blackburn's report was considered by the justices, who invited him to draw up plans for a new prison on a new site. He attended the prison committee in person, and his plans for the Castle Hill site, higher up the town, were adopted in 1788. Thus within three years a newly-built prison was condemned. It was later sold by auction for £1,220. No wonder the Earl of Dorchester, when asked later to sell some land for the approach to the new prison, spoke about 'the removal of the gaol instead of making the former lately built to answer . . . and the very great and unnecessary expense to the city'. There seems real truth in his grumble about lack of foresight and something sadly modern too.

Work on the new gaol, on the site where the present county gaol stands, began in 1790. A loan had to be raised of £10,000 at 4 per cent. The book of subscribers still exists. Morton Pitt invested £1,000. The contract for the new building went to a London builder who was told to effect completion within two years. Again there is a similarity to modern experience: the work fell more and more behind. As late as 1795 the prison committee were still ordering new work and the original contract price had been exceeded.

The new building, finished in 1795, was constructed in six blocks within a strong wall. At the entrance were the keeper's office, committee room, brewhouse and bathhouse incorporated in the wall itself. Inside were the courtyards for the female felons on the left and the female misdemeanants to the right. In the centre block were the keeper's quarters, prisoners' visiting rooms, debtors' day rooms and a number of single cells. Over them on the first floor were the chapel, the cells for condemned and troublesome prisoners, the debtors' sleeping quarters and single sleeping cells. At each corner of the main block, connected to it by an iron bridge, were four smaller blocks of single cells for working and sleeping. By means of seven courtyards, each class of prisoner could be segregated. Storerooms and water-closets were provided on each floor and there was also an infirmary. In one corner of a yard stood a workshop where some interesting but unsuccessful attempts were made to manufacture goods for sale.

According to the ideas of the age, prisoners were classified both by sex and as felons awaiting trial or those convicted and sentenced to imprisonment or transportation. Another category was composed of those imprisoned for breach of contract on bastardy

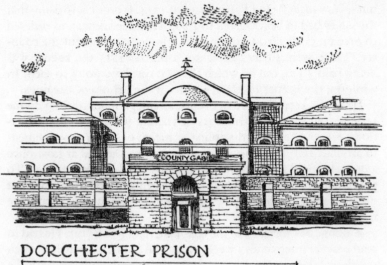

DORCHESTER PRISON

scale 80 FT

orders or for bigamy, vagrants, idle apprentices and servants. The debtors formed another class. All these groups except the debtors were kept, as far as possible, in separate confinement. The new gaol had 88 cells 8½ by 6½ by 9 ft in size. The debtors had a day room and slept at night four to a room; they worked elsewhere. Prisoners condemned to death were lodged in cells near the chapel; near them were some unlighted cells for refractory prisoners in which were large stones with iron rings attached.

Great care was shown, at the outset, in the management of this new prison. The appropriate parliamentary legislation was studied and the committee of management took steps to obtain the regulations for the Gloucestershire gaol from the High Sheriff, who was a follower of Howard's ideas on prison reform. A committee of Dorset justices spent considerable time drawing up a report on the whole question of how the prisoners should be reformed and also how they might contribute to the expenses of the prison.

In charge of the gaol was the keeper; his salary was £150, from which he had to pay two turnkeys. This meagre pay was indeed larger than hitherto, since no longer could the keeper supplement his earnings by selling 'wine, beer, ale or other liquor or to have any beneficial interest or concern whatsoever within the gaol in pursuance of an Act of Parliament' of 1784. It is not surprising that the salary had to be increased to £200 when the keeper was ordered to give up profits from transporting the prisoners about the country. There were further increases, until by 1815 the keeper was being paid £270, out of which the two turnkeys got £50 each. In addition, the keeper received a sixth of the prisoners' earnings.

He had to keep a record of events, attend prisoners during divine service, and enter all particulars of visiting justices' recommendations. He could enforce discipline by means of solitary confinement in an unlit cell, but must visit prisoners so confined at least once a day. He could use irons for particularly troublesome inmates. To prevent escapes, all convicted felons had their clothes removed at night. Above all, the keeper was to 'enforce labour and encourage industry'.

Among the officials was the chaplain, paid £50 a year. He had to read prayers three times a week, preach on Sundays, distribute such religious books as he thought right, 'visit and converse with the prisoners in private as to the state of their minds and give spiritual advice'. He had to keep a record of his observations and also administer a charity fund.

The third official, the surgeon, was less well paid at £30, later increased to £40, out of which he had to provide medicine. He, too, had to prepare an annual report for Quarter Sessions. To help him in an emergency he could employ women prisoners.

From the manuscript records which exist it is possible to draw a picture of the Dorchester prison régime and to fill in some of the details of the administration. Each prisoner was to get a pound and a half of bread at least a day old, from which no bran had been extracted. If they were working they would get extra. During the week 9d worth of meat was allowed. Later, under the pressure of war and the general rise in prices the 9d had to be increased to 2s 6d. Broth, 10d worth, seems to have been part of the extra working ration. Children were fed on a special diet at 3s 6d a week. At Christmas and Whitsun, special meals which cost 6d in 1794 and 1s 5d in 1813 were provided. It is unlikely that the increase in cost meant better meals; it merely reflected the rise in the cost of living. Prisoners in custody awaiting trial were allowed 2s 6d for food and 5d for ale and they could supplement this by buying meat, fish, fruit and pastry. After conviction, the county allowance of bread was substituted.

Sick prisoners were given better food. Tea, gruel and meat diets at 9d appear in the accounts. Only the surgeon could order such food. There is also mention of broth and white bread for children and gin, wine and jellies were given to sick prisoners. One such had 6d worth of wine on twenty-six occasions. Another woman got the same number of doses, which cost 9d each. As she was waiting to be executed she may well have needed the stimulant. When nurses or special guards were employed they too got extra food, 2s 6d worth for a nurse, 5s worth for a midwife and 5s worth when looking after lunatics, several of whom were mentioned in the accounts. There is also the sad entry 'guard over a man who might take his life 1/6 a day and night for 4 months'. This man had been sentenced to transportation and was sent from Dorchester 'to the hulks' at Portsmouth, thence to be shipped overseas. No wonder there was fear that he might commit suicide.

In addition to special diets when ill, the prisoners were given candles or rushlights, poultices costing 3d and bathing in vinegar. Special flannel night shirts were provided 'for those afflicted by itch'. If prisoners died in custody the prison had to pay for their funerals, as also for executions.

To keep the buildings clean, prison wardsmen were appointed to sweep out the cells and to wash them out once a week. Some of the women did this as a form of prison labour. Mops, besoms, long brooms, brushes, soap, candles and coal were all bought under the heading of cleaning. At times gunpowder was used for fumigation and parts of the buildings were lime-washed annually. On admission the men were shaved and bathed at 6d each, the women bathed for 4d. Rat bane, rat traps and the destruction of rats all had to be paid for.

In 1791 it was resolved 'that smock frocks be provided for the convicts employed in work out of the gaol with the letters DORSET GAOL written in legible letters on the back'. A year later there is mention of 'cloth jackets parti-coloured as usual'. Suits of men's and women's clothing were bought. Gaol dresses, aprons, petticoats, smock frocks and bed gowns appear in the accounts, also shoes, shirts, trousers, shifts, hose and clogs. Some of the prison labour was used to make or mend this clothing. It would appear from a report made by some London magistrates who visited in 1816 that a clean shift and shirt were issued weekly. When Elizabeth Rogers was got ready for transportation she was issued with a jacket, gown, three petticoats, two aprons, a handkerchief, a cloak, hat and shoes, in all costing 27s 1d. Rogers and her child had to be sent to Deptford to be put on the transport *Medea*. The journey there cost over £13. It seems strange that she could not be embarked at Portland or Plymouth. Men were sent to Portsmouth until a hulk was stationed at Portland.

Bedding was provided in the cells; iron bedsteads with bed mats which may have been canvas bags stuffed with straw, blankets, rugs, bed-ties, pillowcases and straw were all bought. The blankets had to be washed and mended from time to time. There were chamber pots in the cells.

The keeper had further to account for the purchase of food, furniture, cleaning and nursing within the prison. He had to buy the ledgers in which to keep his records. He bought tape, presumably for mending the clothing, grass seed and thanksgiving books, but why he had to spend 1s 9d on cleaning pistols is not stated. Were the pistols used against the rats? He had to hire carts in which to send the prisoners to and from the courts, pay the turnpike tolls, the ostlers and the guards. He paid '2/- beer for the constables', though the payment of 3s to 'a man to show us the road' seems curious.

Other expenses were incurred when whipping was ordered by a court; this seemed to have cost anything from 4s to 10s. There was a charge when prisoners were ordered to the pillory. The details of an execution in 1807 make sad reading:

| | | | |
|---|---|---|---|
| 7 men watching and guarding the prisoner 84 nights at 2/- | 8 | 8 | 0 |
| Bread and wine for the Sacrament | | 4 | 6 |
| Ropes | | 3 | 2 |
| Executioner's fee | 5 | 5 | 0 |
| Victuals and beer for the guards | 1 | 1 | 0 |
| Extra turnkey | | 10 | 0 |
| 6 men on the day of execution to keep the people from injuring the potatoes | | 6 | 0 |
| Setting up and taking down the drop | | 10 | 6 |
| 6 watchmen 29 nights at 2/- | 2 | 18 | 0 |
| | 19 | 6 | 2 |

The item about the people on the day of execution is a reminder that executions were in public; they took place on the flat roof of the entrance lodge in view of all criminal prisoners, who were brought from their cells, doubtless to benefit from the lesson of the occasion. It is interesting that when the woman Cook was hanged in 1814 for murder, it was ordered that after execution her body 'be dissected and anatomised'. She was executed at 1.30 pm and the body was handed over to the surgeon.

The total cost of running the prison varied from nearly £800 in 1793–4 to £3,446 12s 6½d in 1807, but it usually amounted to between one and two thousand pounds. A comparison with the total county expenditure shows that the prison costs were the largest single item and came to nearly a quarter of the total. The war on crime was not cheap.

It was to offset this expenditure, as well as to afford a measure of reform, that attempts were made to arrange employment. 'We do not hesitate', wrote the justices in 1800, 'to pronounce that this expense (the maintenance of the prison) may be nearly if not wholly annihilated. We cannot help observing that in a moral and political point of view, its benefits can hardly be estimated.' Four trades, timber, details of which are not given, hatting, making nets and mops were to be carried on in the old prison. If a man were sentenced to hard labour two-thirds of the profits were to go to the county fund, a sixth to the keeper 'as an inducement to be attentive'. Of the remaining sixth, part was to be paid to the prisoner in gaol and part kept until his release. Modern penal practice follows this very closely, though the governor today does not benefit. If a man were not sentenced to hard labour his share rose to half. The accounts for the next sixteen years show a loss on this prison work in two of them, and profits on the others ranging from just over £89 to a year in which £315 11s 8½d was made.

It would seem that more and more attention was given to the hatting trade. Morton Pitt paid for a special building in one of the yards. A debtor, George Wiffin, was put in charge and at first gave so much satisfaction that he was voted ten guineas reward. Within three years he began to neglect the business, then appeared to have absconded and a prosecution was undertaken. This may explain the fact that a loss was made during his control. His place was then taken by a civilian hat-maker from Bridport. This appointment, too, seems to have lasted only four or five years, since Morton Pitt was engaged in 1801 in finding a new superintendent of the hatting. In December of that year Thomas Lowe, 'recommended by some of the most respectable houses in London for sobriety honesty and knowledge', was appointed at £60 a year; he had to provide his own lodgings. It seems that difficulty was experienced in collecting the money owing for hats, and the keeper had to request payment on several occasions. Despite more and more capital invested in the trade, it was decided to abandon it in 1808. No reasons are given, but it looks as though the optimistic hope that it would cover the cost of maintaining the prison was never realized.

When the new prison was being built, men laboured at paving, road-making, hedging and turf-cutting. They cleaned snow from the roofs. Others worked at tailoring, carpentry, weaving, shoe-making, netting and carding. At one time there was a basket-maker at work, another made clocks, another harness, while one prisoner was paid for sweeping chimneys. Probably a craftsman was allowed to continue his craft. The women prisoners spun, made shirts, mats and nets, lined hats, knitted, washed, cleaned and nursed. There appears to have been no distinction between the type of work and the sentence being served, whether hard labour, imprisonment, awaiting transportation or detention for want of sureties. Debtors and those awaiting trial were all employed.

The costs of the prison rose steadily, owing partly to rising war prices and partly to an increase in the number committed to gaol. In 1779 there were 20 in custody, in 1801 109, and during the troubled years immediately after the Napoleonic Wars there were 126 for the Christmas dinner. As in modern times, far more men went to prison than women.

What crimes had they committed? The Dorset prison records reflect the national situation, harsh and unrelenting. Generally the death sentence was remitted to periods of transportation either for life or for seven or fourteen years. When John Higham was executed in 1801 for highway robbery he had already served a previous sentence for stealing a watch. Several prisoners appear more than once in the records. Ambrose Ridout, aged 22, was sentenced to a month's hard labour for stealing a deer. Two years later he was again deer-stealing and got a year. No sooner was he out then he committed burglary for which he was transported for life. George House and John Bailey both assaulted the Customs and Excise Officers and got two years. Later House broke open a barn and Bailey hunted deer and landed up in prison again.

The same crime appears to have had different punishments, but of course the records do not show the circumstances in which the offence took place. Sheep-stealing could be punished by five or seven years' hard labour; housebreaking by five years or two years and a fine of 6d, stealing silver spoons by two years' hard labour or one year with a fine of 1s. Some of the punishments were, by modern standards, savage in the extreme: three years' hard labour for stealing fowls, one year for stealing a greatcoat, six months for a joint of mutton. When Ann Curtis, who was only nine, stole a pair of pattens she was reprimanded and acquitted on account of her youth, but Ann Barrett, a year older, was not so lucky. She stole a piece of linen and was fined and sentenced to a year in gaol. William Valentine, only twelve, stole in a dwelling-house and was sentenced to death; this was remitted to seven years' transportation. The theft of a handkerchief meant a year's hard labour for fifteen-year-old Samuel Thompson. Rebecca Gillinham, two years older, was a receiver of stolen goods. She was sentenced to fourteen years' transportation, remitted to hard labour. For seven years she worked as a spinner and at lining hats. Evidently she was industrious, since she was then pardoned 'on account of good behaviour'. There are several examples of such remissions. Others were discharged on condition that they entered the Army or Navy. Joseph Warr, aged twenty-four, stole money. He appeared 'a true penitent and voluntarily remains in prison until an opportunity offers for him to go abroad in His Majesty's Service'. In the next year Warr enlisted in a regiment of foot and went abroad. The Duke of Wellington's opinion that he commanded an army of ex-convicts is certainly borne out by the Dorset records. Thomas Burne, who committed a breach of the peace, went to the local regiment. John Quinn, eighteen, and Flan Ward, fifty-five, were excused the death sentence for robbery if they enlisted to serve on the coast of Africa. Many thus 'enlisted'. They were a mixed collection: the prison comments on their characters showed them to be 'industrious but somewhat disorderly', 'orderly and industrious', 'industrious but often sick' or 'a very lazy fellow'.

The remarks column in the annual reports seems to illustrate very great faith in the curative value of prison. In the main the prisoners are described as 'orderly and industrious', at times even 'uniformly exemplary' or 'apparently reclaimed'. Those who did not seem to benefit were labelled 'most disorderly', or 'somewhat disorderly' or 'an artful, disorderly man' (a bigamist this one) or a woman 'industrious but of an abandoned mind'. Was she mentally defective or a lunatic?

Elizabeth Rogers has already been mentioned in connexion with the clothes that had to be bought for her. She was nineteen in 1794, when she was committed for housebreaking and sentenced to death. This was remitted to seven years' transportation. She was put to spinning until the summer of 1796, when she worked as a cleaner. She had been labelled 'disorderly' in the first report on her. It was not until the spring of 1797 that she was sent to Deptford for transportation. Generally a considerable period elapsed between sentence and transportation itself. Lydia Parker was kept for three years in Dorchester before being sent to New South Wales. Presumably the women could not be sent to the 'hulks' as the male convicts were.

Public whippings were administered to young men and women convicted of theft, and everything seems to have been stolen; sheep, deer, horses, asses and pigs, money, watches, spoons, corn, bread, meat, bees, poultry, clothes, shoes, wood, furniture, flax and nets. Murder and highway robbery were committed, housebreaking, assaults, conspiracy, bigamy, sodomy, counterfeiting; men embezzled, swindled, stole a wreck, damaged a ship, left their families, broke their apprenticeship, offended against the revenue and the game laws, smuggled, received stolen goods and threatened to set fire to houses. Desertions from the Army rose until, in 1813, thirteen men were returned to their regiments. In the previous year four escaped French prisoners of war were handed over by the authorities to a sergeant of the 39th Regiment of Foot to be conducted under escort to Gosport.

An idea of the amount of crime in the county can be estimated from the records of a single year, 1802–3. This may not, of course, be completely typical. In it 44 men and women were already under sentence and 113 men and 28 women were tried—making a total of 185. In 1803–4 the total had risen to 214. The problems of a crime wave are not new. In the first year under review twenty-eight crimes were classified; the greatest number were of begging by vagrants and various kinds of theft. Some of those convicted were not Dorset men, but the majority were. The fact that more and more were imprisoned is a reflection of the political and economic background of the times. Owing to the coincidence of wars and the

15. Early Purbeck marble monument

16. Pyemore Mills, near Bridport

17. Former silk mill, Sherborne

agrarian and industrial revolutions, standards of real wages were dropping and there was much unemployment in the countryside. The Poor Law system was breaking down under pressure and there was restlessness and great uneasiness everywhere. Anti-enclosure riots and mutinies in the Navy made magistrates quicker to act and to enforce the new legislation against poachers. This may account for the harshness of the sentences; to commit a boy of fifteen to seven years in Australia for stealing a pair of boots or another for taking a pair of stockings, or a man of fifty-eight for stealing a halfpenny shows the law at its worst. In 1816 many turned poacher, which must have reflected the uneasiness after the war ended, the recession in agriculture and the evil results of the Corn Laws. The keep of Cranborne Chase was beaten up. Food of all sorts was stolen; deer, turnips, cheese, fowls and potatoes; pointers to the hungriness of the countryside as much as to its lawlessness. Men were taken for smuggling. Men and women rioted in Bridport.

Now and then prison records reveal some touches of humanity. There were a few local philanthropists, among them Morton Pitt and Earl and Countess Digby, who contributed to a small fund which the chaplain administered. From it he might give a little money to a prisoner on discharge. Joseph Warr got half a guinea when he enlisted. Sometimes clothing was bought for a man going out. One man had £1 14s 10d spent on him, with 6s 6d for his carriage to Poole.

How far was the new prison in Dorchester a model one run exactly as Howard suggested? When there were more than eighty-eight convicts there the principle of solitary confinement had to be abandoned. Where Howard asked for two clean shirts a week, only one was provided. The cells were slightly less high than he advocated and it is doubtful if they were lime-washed twice a year as he wanted. There were the hot baths and provision for baking verminous clothing, and the beds and bedding that he wanted. The bread ration came up to his standard, but whereas he wanted half a pound of boiled meat on Sundays, this seems only to have been provided at Whitsun and Christmas. There is no mention of the daily penny for cheese, butter, potatoes, peas and turnips. Nevertheless the prisoners did earn a little money, so perhaps they bought vegetables. Certainly water for washing them was provided in one of the courts.

The magistrates visited the gaol regularly: the keeper and the surgeon both furnished their annual reports. It would seem, in fact, that a very real effort was made under Morton Pitt's direction to carry out Howard's recommendations and it is perhaps not a coincidence that a copy of the 1790 edition of his *State of the Prisons* was tied up with the manuscript papers relating to the building of the new gaol, together with the keeper's accounts, quarter by quarter, duly audited by two justices, which show that these at least were prepared to accept responsibility for the prison under their care, for financial if not for humane reasons.

# CHAPTER NINE

## Lunatic asylums in the county 1774–1850

The eighteenth century saw some slight improvement in the care of lunatics. In Queen Anne's reign legislation was passed whereby pauper lunatics were no longer classed with vagabonds; two justices of the peace could order their confinement. Whipping them was forbidden. There was, however, little provision for places in which they could be confined. Outside London few hospitals existed, but there were some private madhouses. In 1763 a committee was set up to enquire into the state of these establishments, which resulted, in 1774, in a system of statutory licensing. No person could keep more than one lunatic without entering into a recognisance of £100, with two sureties of £50 each, with the justices at Quarter Sessions; the licence itself was to cost from £10 to £15, according to the number of lunatics to be lodged. Once a year a magistrate and a physician were to inspect the establishment between the hours of eight and five during the day. No person was to be admitted to the house except with a doctor's written order, and the keeper had to notify the admission within three days. Failure to report or to license was to be heavily fined; cases of cruelty were to be dealt with by common law.

There were obvious weaknesses in this legislation, since there was no power to withhold or revoke licences and the hours and amount of inspection were very limited. C. W. W. Wynn, a vigorous humanitarian, succeeded in 1807 in having another Select Committee appointed to which Romilly and Wilberforce, among others, gave evidence which suggested that the problems of private madhouses were underestimated. There were often more lunatics admitted than the registers suggested and there was great need for the erection of such pauper asylums as existed in York, Liverpool and elsewhere. Wynn's Act of 1808 gave counties permission to erect such asylums, but only ten did so in the following twenty years. In 1828, therefore, an important new Act was passed 'to regulate the care and treatment of insane persons'. Under it there were to be fifteen Commissioners in Lunacy, of which five were to be physicians. They had powers both to license, granted as hitherto at Quarter Sessions, and to visit and inspect at all hours of the day or night. The justices in their turn were to visit at least four times a year and send an annual report to the Secretary of State. Houses with a hundred or more inmates must have a resident physician, smaller establishments must be visited by a doctor twice a week. Careful details of the inmates, by whom consigned, name, occupation, age, by whom certified and the success or failure of treatment must be kept in a special register.

One of the most famous of Dorset men, Anthony Ashley Cooper, later Lord Shaftesbury, was one of these fifteen Commissioners in Lunacy, and among the county records are registers of several private lunatic asylums from which it is possible to see how the Acts of 1774 and 1828 were implemented and to trace the establishment of the first county asylum for pauper lunatics under the second Act.

The first private lunatic asylum in Dorset of which records exist was kept by John Mercer at Halstock. Part of the original buildings still exist and are now incorporated into a private house. The Mercers were medical men for several generations. John Mercer, son of a doctor, married Lydia White of Evershot and died in 1782. After his death his brother Justinian, a surgeon, ran the establishment until 1809. John Mercer, grandson of the first John, also a surgeon, looked after Halstock for the next eight years. He died when only thirty-five, whereupon his widow, Alice, helped by her Aunt Betsy, Justinian's daughter, was in charge of the asylum until 1839 when Alice's son Justinian, another surgeon, was old enough to take over. The house was still an asylum when the Lunacy Commissioners reported in 1847, but there is no mention of it in the 1850 report.

There is a local tradition that John Mercer opened his establishment to care for an insane member of a neighbouring family of landed gentry. The Mercers were well known in Halstock. They were churchwardens, rented several properties and no doubt served as doctors to the surrounding country. It was stated at Quarter Sessions when John applied for his fresh licence that he had 'for many years past kept a house for the reception of lunatics'.

This was Portland House in Halstock. The first entries in the register to be kept under the 1774 Act show six lunatics lodged there, four men aged seventy, thirty-six, twenty-six and fifteen, and two women of thirty-six and thirty-two. It is interesting that all were from the neighbouring counties of Somerset and Devon. The first inspection of the establishment recorded 'all lunatics clean and in decent apparel and well accommodated with all necessaries of life . . . [the house is] situated in exceedingly healthy country and kept in good order'. Over the years the number lodged at Halstock increased to nearly thirty. After the opening of the County Asylum it began to fall until at the end a mere handful were there.

Either Mercer's establishment was good of its kind or there were very few such houses, for the inmates came from as far afield as Penzance, Brighton and London, as well as from the neighbouring counties. They were consigned there by wives, husbands, fathers, mothers, brothers, sisters, uncles, trustees and even one, Pretor Pinny, entered on his own account in 1809 when he was twenty-eight. There he remained till his death twenty years later. Others were lodged in the house by the Poor Law officers. In 1812, of the twenty-three inmates, eight were paupers coming from such distances as Portland and Swanage. The Buckland Newton Poor Law accounts contain the bills for Ann Buckler, lodged in Halstock in 1797. £1 1s 0d was paid as an entrance fee and 14s a week thereafter. Curiously enough, when Joseph Whitrow was sent there in 1816 from Kimmeridge he only cost 7s, later reduced to 5s. Perhaps the rates were reduced, as he stayed there over eight years. This was quite a short stay compared with that of William Spong, a single gentleman from Wimborne, who was fifty when he was admitted and who died twenty-six years later. Another man, John Toogood, a labourer, was there a year longer. The Mercers seem to have been willing to accept lunatics of any age; among the oldest admitted was Thomas Noakes, aged seventy-five, and Jane Stephens, widow, seventy, while George Hunt at fifteen was the youngest. The patients had varied family backgrounds; a vicar, Edward Philips of Montacute, and other gentlemen, a lieutenant in the Royal Navy, an Army captain, a medical man, a chemist and druggist appear. All types of craftsmen went mad; tallow chandler, currier, cooper, shoemaker, joiner, mason, mercer, butcher, blacksmith; all were consigned there. Among the women servants, mantua makers and milliners needed asylum. In 1821 Thomas Barret and Samuel Hopkins 'escaped last night through the roof of the House and have not yet been found, but search is being made for them by proper persons'. In the next year the doctor reported that one of the inmates had gone on a visit to Exeter. As however the doctor met him 'at the Inn' it would seem that the journey was being broken for refreshment.

After 1828 the Halstock register is more interesting, since the visitors give more details. They note on one occasion that four male patients are under restraint in the daytime and two women also. Others have to be restrained at night. How is not described; an attempt will be made later in this chapter to suggest the various methods in use elsewhere. One of the women 'remains constantly in bed'. Two others appear convalescent, and it was suggested that Mrs Mercer should write to their friends to consider the propriety of removing them. The visitors consider that there is not enough space for exercise and manual labour. A bath, too, is needed. This reflects current ideas on treatment. When the warm bath was provided at Halstock it had a beneficial effect. The visitors were careful to note that, while there was no religious service at the asylum itself, two of the inmates were well enough to go to the parish church. Of the twenty-five inmates reported on in 1829, twenty were considered incurable; one, Joseph Foss, a Chideock fisherman, committed suicide and two others died. The visitors were tart in their comments on Joseph Foss, who had escaped before he hanged himself. They were of 'the opinion that blame is attached to the Keeper of this Asylum for having permitted to this man the full use of his hands. Immediate search was made for him by several persons but without effect although he was missed within ten minutes of his escape.'

The visitors turn their attention to food and bedding. They suggest in 1830 that each patient be supplied with two good top blankets and one under blanket during winter. They recommend the use of chloride of lime in the different wards twice in hot weather and usually once. They suggest that a shed be erected immediately in the court of the women's ward, to protect the patients from the influence of the sun and rain. They are pleased when they can note that 'the prayers of the church are clearly read to such patients as are deemed capable of receiving consolation therefrom'. In 1838 'one female of advanced years and indolent habits has been indisposed because she refused to leave her bedroom'. The visitors sternly recommend that she be removed to a sitting-room for some hours daily.

Two other private lunatic homes had been opened in Dorset, one at Broadhays House in the parish of Stockland in 1829 by William Spicer—this was slightly larger than Portland House— and another small one taking three patients at Cranborne, keeper William Symes. The visitors' comments are much as for Halstock. They were annoyed to find no Sunday prayers at Broadhays and request that the surgeon make his report 'more explicit and more satisfactory'. The bedding is not sufficiently warm. At Cranborne the windows should be secured by iron bars to prevent a patient from throwing himself out. The magistrates are worried about the food at Broadhays. Where the pauper lunatics are concerned the keeper is using the dietary scale of the Axminster Poor Law Union which the visitors feel is not adapted or sufficient for lunatics whose bodily health is good. If they are in good health they work on the farm daily. They have also a skittle alley 'which in fine weather is much resorted to by the patients', who also have access to newspapers and books. Some attempt seems to have been made to classify patients at Broadhays. An escape occurred over a twelve-foot wall and on another occasion a patient wrenched the iron bar from a window and two got out. The visitors were worried by the poor clothing of the pauper inmates who were 'very insufficiently and hardly decently clad'. Because of complaints about the food from some of the more intelligent patients to whom the visitors spoke, the latter inspected a dinner which appeared sufficient. They wanted the pauper inmates separated from the boarders. That there were still paupers in private establishments as late as 1839 was probably due to the demand on the County Pauper Asylum. One wonders how wise the visitors were in recommending the discharge of one patient, Elizabeth Aplin, who, though much improved, was 'still not free from all visionary ideas'. On a visit to Broadhays in April 1840, they were indignant to find both manager and keeper absent and all the male patients locked up together.

There is mention of the Dorset establishments in the Metropolitan Commissioner's report of 1844. Under legislation of the previous year an increase had been made in the number of commissioners who were now to visit all licensed houses. There were now only ten patients at Halstock, seven men and three women;

one of the latter was thought to be curable, one man was an epileptic. At Cranborne there were six inmates, half of whom were deemed incurable. The Commissioners subdivided the patients into upper and middle class, of whom there were seven at Halstock and three at Cranborne; the remainder were labelled artisan. The metropolitan visitors reported that Mr Mercer 'seemed kindly disposed towards his people but the rooms occupied by two of them have been reported upon at our different visits as defective in every respect. At our last visit they were described as low, dirty and without any furniture except a wooden bedstead'. Things were worse at Cranborne, which was visited three times in one year. At the third visit—

> the Proprietor was absent 30 miles from Cranborne having left home on the Tuesday and not expected to return until Friday. There was no Superintendent, Keeper or Nurse to take charge of the patients and there was only one female servant and a boy, 16 years old in the House. We were told there was a farming man who might be sent for in case any of the patients should be violent. A female who resides in an adjoining house comes to the Asylum daily and presides at meals and assists in the Establishment. There was also a female who had been a patient, and was still a Boarder in the House who assisted in the management of it. The Proprietor of this House had not been at home at any one of the visits of the Commissioners. If the engagements of the Proprietor of an Asylum take him so frequently and for such long periods from home some responsible and competent person ought, we think, to be left in charge of the Patients.

Both establishments, Halstock and Cranborne, were still taking patients in 1849; indeed there were eight in each. The fifth annual report of the Commissioners, in 1850, has no mention of Cranborne, and of Halstock simply a note that it was formerly licensed to Mr Mercer. 'There are no provincial licensed houses for Dorset.' Perhaps this was just as well.

### The county asylum and the treatment of lunatics

In the early years of the nineteenth century reformers like Wynn and Romilly were hard at work. The permissive legislation of 1808 enabled county authorities to set up lunatic asylums. Visits made to older establishments at York and Bethlem revealed frightful conditions; a Member of Parliament, Edward Wakefield, discovered William Norris in Bethlem confined in an iron collar in a cell where he had been for ten years; some others were lying naked on straw. Revelations at the York Asylum were just as horrible. After difficulty in getting some cells unlocked—it was said the key was lost—the visitors found four cells eight feet square, squalid and filthy, with the walls bedaubed with excrement. Into them thirteen women were locked at night. By day the women were herded into a room upstairs twelve feet by seven. There was reason to believe that the keepers concealed the deaths of many lunatics. This and other evidence was published in the report of a Select Committee in 1816. The reformers worked on. Eleven years later another Select Committee was responsible for further legislation. The County Asylum Bill was introduced by Ashley in a maiden speech. He was supported by Robert Gordon, Wynn and Charles Wood. This became the Act of 1828 already referred to, which set up the Commissioners in Lunacy with greater powers of licensing and inspection. It also encouraged the founding of more county pauper asylums.

Dorset, while not availing itself of the permissive legislation of 1808, was beginning to consider the problem of pauper lunatics shortly before the County Asylum Act became law. At the Michaelmas Quarter Sessions of 1827 the justices of Petty Sessions were ordered to seek information from the Poor Law overseers as to how many lunatics and dangerous idiots they had in their care. A notice in local newspapers in December spoke of the intention of the authorities to provide a county asylum. A generous gift from one of the county Members, F. J. Browne of Forston House, helped the project. In addition to the house, standing on the main Dorchester–Charminster road with seven acres of ground, Mr Browne gave the handsome sum of £4,000 invested in Consols. Forston House, which can still be seen, served as part of the County Asylum until the mid-century when it was moved to Herrison House near by.

More money was needed to get Forston House in order and to provide additional buildings. All the notables of the county responded to the appeal. Lord Digby gave £200, Lord Ilchester £100, Lord Shaftesbury £100—the list exists of almost £3,000 raised by donations. William Evans of Wimborne was engaged as architect. He was instructed to visit an asylum at Laverstock, near Salisbury, and to confer with Dr Finch there about the plans for the additions. William Morton Pitt was elected chairman of the committee to consider the plans for the asylum, which was to be sufficient for forty inmates. This was shortly increased to sixty when plans for the buildings were approved. Two wings were added to Forston House at a cost of £5,320, the scullery and out-houses were adapted, privies, pumps, exercise grounds, wash, brew and bakehouses were built, a boundary wall was constructed, with various cottages and bridges, and alterations were made to the gardens and river course. All these came to over £12,000. In addition furniture and apparel for the patients, furniture for keepers and nurses, and medical stores had to be bought. When the subscriptions had been deducted from the outlay, the sum of £10,753 17s 3d had to be met. This was raised by loans on security of the county rates, to be paid off by instalments, and by a weekly boarding rate of 8s 9d per pauper admitted. It speaks well for the committee that the loans were paid off within seven years.

The original buildings soon proved too small. More cells and a steam apparatus for warming had to be added and other rooms enlarged. As time went on changes in the classification of patients meant changes of building, and changes in treatment also resulted in additional expenditure.

While the architect was at work, advertisements appeared inviting applications for the post of superintendent; he had to be an experienced medical man of 'unexceptional character'. Some of these applications still exist, including one from Dr Symes of Cranborne who later wished to withdraw since he had decided 'to continue my present situation'. Perhaps the salary of £140 did not appeal to him. His sister, aged thirty-two, had applied for the post of matron at £50 a year. Others who applied were L. G. Giles, house apothecary and secretary of Winchester County Hospital, Mr Langstaff from Wilton Infirmary and Thomas Fisher from Nottingham Lunatic Asylum. Among the applicants for matron was Miss White Parsons, who stated her age to be 'between 40 and 50'. She was warmly supported by Dr Finch, who said that 'Miss Parsons' family connexions are very respectable but through the imprudence or worse than imprudent conduct of her brothers she had been reduced to seek means of supporting herself'. Poor Miss Parsons. There is a particularly nice touch in the application of Lydia Dodd, matron at Weymouth, who said 'it would be presumptuous in me to write in my own praise'.

A dietary for the inmates was drawn up:

> Breakfast—milk porridge and 6 ounces of bread
> Dinner—2 days. 6 ounces cooked meat and vegetables
>       2 days. 1 pound suet or rice pudding
>       2 days. Soup and 6 ounces of bread
>       1 day. Bread and cheese.
>             Ale with dinner daily.
> Supper—6 ounces of bread, 2 ounces of cheese with Ale.
> Patients who are actively employed to have extra.

This is a diet on workhouse lines, dull and meagre. In 1840 it was slightly changed. A pound of suet pudding was served on Fridays and pie crust with half a pound of potatoes and six ounces of meat on Saturdays. The allowance of beer was half a pint. Women were to get an ounce less bread than the men and if they 'made themselves generally useful could have tea and butter if preferred'.

The rules for the establishment were comprehensive. The asylum visitors were to meet when it was deemed necessary, but always just before Quarter Sessions. They were to furnish quarterly reports, many of which still exist, and an annual report too. They were further empowered to give orders to the staff. The superintendent had to devote himself fully to his post, visit every ward and patient at least once a day, treat them with the greatest humanity and kindness and personally examine from time to time the beds, linen and clothing of every male patient. He alone could order restraint and must make a note of such treatment. He was expected to keep a day book, a register, a medical journal on treatment, a visitors' book, a parish account book and a cash book. Should he wish to be absent for more than one night he must get written permission from two visitors. With so much to do, occasional leave must have been almost essential.

The matron had to see every female patient once a day, superintend the weighing out of the food and soap, oversee the kitchens, dairy and stores, cut out the women's clothing and direct its making, inspect the beds and keep the inventories. As far as they were capable she could employ the female patients with gentleness and kindness. She would surely need help, too.

There was a chaplain to conduct Divine Service every Sunday in a hut decently and appropriately furnished and to attend any patients when the superintendent advised. The patients were allowed visitors with the superintendent's permission, but they must not bring money, wine, tobacco, snuff, books, fruit, cakes or sweetmeats, except with his agreement. There is a flavour of a prison régime here. The overseers of the poor could at all times see those for whom they were responsible. Deaths were to be notified immediately.

The daily pattern of the inmates' lives was clearly defined. On admission they were to be carefully examined. Their hair was to be cut and cleansed by the keepers. Every day the keepers were to get up at six o'clock in summer, seven in winter and get the patients up too, washing and combing them, ascertaining their health and paying a strict regard to cleanliness. Breakfast was at eight. At an early hour the keepers were to clean out the galleries and bedrooms, open the beds and hang the bedding to air, remove wet straw, dirt or dirty linen, and in suitable weather open the windows. An hour before meals the keepers were to take their trays to the kitchen and also collect medicines from the surgery. Patients were to assist the cook and kitchenmaid in washing up. Every knife, fork and spoon was to be counted and then locked up. The patients were to go to bed shortly after seven o'clock supper. How they filled in the rest of their time will be described later. Twice a week the keepers were to shave the men. The keepers were never to leave their wards unless on urgent business, and then having notified another keeper and locked up any patients likely to be violent. Fines for a first offence were to be imposed if a keeper struck or ill-treated a patient; dismissal followed a second lapse. They must keep themselves 'decently clean in their persons, decorous in their behaviour', accept neither presents nor gratuities nor sell anything to the patients. If a patient escaped owing to a keeper's negligence the latter must bear the whole cost of recapturing the escaper. The keepers were also liable to be fined if they failed to lock up instruments and tools. Altogether theirs seems to have been a taxing life. From a letter written by Dr Button, superintendent in 1843, it seems that there were two male attendants at £30 a year, two at £25, two female keepers at £15 and two at £12. The cook got £15, the housemaid and the laundrymaid both £12, a kitchenmaid £10. The gardener was paid £30, the stoker £20, the gardener's wife who acted as portress at the lodge £5. Dr Button himself, with the Diplomas of Apothecaries Hall and the College of Surgeons, was paid £170. The matron's salary remained unchanged at £50, while the non-resident chaplain also got £50. It cannot be said that Dorset was lavish in its salary scales.

What kind of men and women were lodged in the hospital and what had caused their illnesses? An analysis of the thirty-seven patients admitted in 1843 showed twenty-one men and sixteen women ranging in age from one of nine years old, a congenital idiot, to a man of eighty-one suffering for thirty years from dementia, the cause of which was not known. The classification of illness covered mania, dementia, melancholia, monomania and general paralysis of the insane. Among the causes of such illnesses were poverty, grief, disappointed hope, heredity, intemperance, pecuniary difficulties, childbirth, injury to the head, anxiety, and in the case of one young man, 'over study'. Generally speaking the patients accepted in 1843 had only been suffering from their illnesses for a few months. Time and time again the medical superintendents in their reports begged that patients should be sent to hospital quickly when there was hope of recovery. Not only did the 1843 report deal with illness and its cause, but the patients were also carefully classified as to education; three were well-educated, eleven could read and write, ten could read and three were illiterate. The majority were members of the Church of England but there were two Baptists, two Independents, two Ranters and two 'unknown'.

There are many glimpses in the annual reports of the patients and their symptoms. Several tried to commit suicide by drowning, hanging, even by trying to swallow a sheet. 'The devil tells me to do it,' said one man; he was treated with sedatives and his hands were restrained. Some refused food, believing it to be poisoned. In one case a woman said she was 'unworthy' to be fed. Some would only eat by stealth or refused a certain kind of food. One man believed pork to be human flesh. Another had the devil in his stomach which made his appetite voracious. Another believed himself to be dead as his head had been cut off and dead people could not eat. One poor man with general paralysis suffered from the delusion that he had gold in the bank and owned a splendid coach. Two women thought themselves God and each disputed the rule of the other with such vigour that they had to be separated. There was belief in witchcraft—having been 'overlooked'. The causes of illness were graded under the headings of moral causes, anxiety and the like, including religious excitement, and physical causes, epilepsy, typhus, injuries to the head. Intemperance 'especially prevalent among sailors', was deemed a moral cause of disorder.

Whenever possible patients were employed in the hospital. Because most of the patients had been agricultural labourers it was noted that they became listless and dull when unemployed. Manual labour was therefore held to be both a mental and a muscular means to quietness. The men worked in the garden where they grew potatoes, carrots, cabbages and onions; in the stables; tailoring, about the wards, attending the boiler and on mechanical work like picking flock and horsehair or breaking bones for manure. They sawed wood, made mats for use in the wards, looked after pigs and cows and helped to brew the asylum ale. They did shoemaking— Lancashire clogs for the gaol or leather shoes and boots. The women worked in the kitchen, wards and laundry. They made gowns, petticoats, shifts, sheets, pillowcases, aprons, capes for themselves and jackets and trousers for the men. They knitted stockings and plaited straw bonnets, some for a charity school, some for the prison and others for themselves. A very modern note is struck by the complaint 'it is regretted that sufficient market cannot be found for such articles as could be made'. A little profit was made from the sale of these articles which provided a fund from which to supply inmates with tea and tobacco and a small sum of money on discharge.

Work therapy was supported by attempts to encourage amusements. A library with newspapers was provided and one patient at least would frequently exclaim: 'Please sir, give it to me, it keeps me quiet you know.' It was *The Times*. The *Dorset County Chronicle*, *Chambers' Journal* and *The Saturday Magazine* were also read. One woman was taught to read by her fellows. The day room was decorated with prints, drawings and plants in pots. A New Year entertainment was attended by sixty patients; there was music and singing and each had a piece of cake and a glass of warm elder wine made from berries collected by the women. At harvest the women went gleaning and enjoyed cakes baked from the corn.

There was a room set aside for Divine Service, but it was so small that patients had to take turns. This was deplored, since it was 'highly gratifying to witness the deep and earnest attention which is generally manifest by this little congregation. The degree of self-control during the hour is far from being the principal advantage derived from it. No doubt higher and holier feelings are called into exercise'.

There was, however, another side to the picture. Restraint, while regulated and reported, had often to be used. At Herrison House a collection of instruments of mechanical restraint still exists. There are metal handcuffs, padded leather cuffs, and leather muffs which cover the whole hand and can be strapped to body or bed. There are belts with handcuffs, belts with leather sleeves that restrain the whole arm, ankle cuffs and several varieties of very heavy leather harness. These, weighing eight or ten pounds, were used out of doors, since patients so clothed could wheel barrows while not lifting their arms to any height. There are strong suits in existence, where the laced fastenings are at the back, and heavy double-stitched canvas blankets which defied destruction. The spoons used for forcible feeding, shaped like a tube with a hole at one end, exist, as do the solid, non-stabbing forks with very short prongs and the knives with only an inch of blade. In this collection of relics are some patient-made keys, knives and screwdrivers.

Treatment of the patients was not only 'moral', that is through work and amusement, but also medical. Emetics, strong purges and drugs were used. In an appendix to the 1847 Report of the Lunacy Commissioners there is a section devoted to the work of Dr Button, Dorset Superintendent. For the treatment of mania he used blood-letting by means of leeches or cupping behind the ears, on the forehead or at the nape of the neck. He applied cold poultices to the shaven head and warmth to the feet. He believed in counter-irritants, blistering the nape of the neck or applying tartar antimony to the shorn scalp. Antimony was also used as an emetic. Among sedatives he used preparations of opium, salts of morphia or camphor. Warm baths were useful, as was a nourishing diet.

Often nineteenth-century treatments to induce nausea, though not specifically mentioned, were in use at Forston House; these included swinging and rotating machines in which the violent action produced sickness. Sometimes patients were totally enclosed in a bath except for their heads. Convulsive and electrical shock treatments were also favoured. No wonder tonics, sedatives and a nourishing diet were also prescribed to keep the patients alive.

Dr Button's treatments seem to be in line with the general practice of the mid-century. In the 1844 Report Dorset claimed that over the previous five years 52·9 per cent cures had been effected, which compared favourably with other authorities. It is probable that these were highly optimistic figures. Since the cost of maintenance was 6s 5d weekly, rising to 7s at times, the nourishing diet of good quality must have been also somewhat illusory.

The breakdown of the 7s charged to the parish in 1847 is as follows:

|                    | s | d                |
| ------------------ | - | ---------------- |
| Provisions         | 3 | $2\frac{3}{8}$   |
| House expenses     | 1 | $7\frac{1}{8}$   |
| Clothing           |   | 6                |
| Salaries and wages | 1 | $4\frac{1}{2}$   |
| Medicine           |   | $6\frac{1}{2}$   |
|                    | 7 | $2\frac{1}{2}$   |

That the Dorset magistrates and the medical superintendents did their duty according to the standards of the time is undeniable, and the task was no easy one. Idiots and the senile, men and women curable and incurable, and even criminal lunatics were sent to the County Asylum from the parishes. They were sometimes received too late for help and in a sad state. One such admitted 'had been for several years almost without clothing in an outhouse with a blanket to cover her'. Her daughter took her food but nothing else was done for her. Only after long courses of bleeding, blistering and purging had failed were paupers sometimes sent to the asylum 'exhausted and enfeebled'. The Commissioners visiting in 1844 commented on the cleanliness and absence of offensive smell in all parts of the hospital. 'The patients were quiet and tranquil and most of them cheerful and comfortable. None under mechanical restraint. Such restraint very rarely used.' The food for the females' dinner was liberal and of good quality. 'The condition of the whole establishment reflects great credit on those to whom the management and supervision is committed.' They were, however, worried about the dampness and some lack of security against escape. Indeed patients did escape. The gardener, having allowed one to do so for the second time, had to pay £2. On another occasion one Nehemiah Masefield escaped back to his parish, in his asylum clothes. When the keeper arrived his family refused to give him up. The village constable then had to arrest him; one wonders whether for the theft of the clothing or for his greater safety.

# CAUTION.

WHEREAS it has been represented to us from several quarters, that mischievous and designing Persons have been for some time past, endeavouring to induce, and have induced, many Labourers in various Parishes in this County, to attend Meetings, and to enter into Illegal Societies or Unions, to which they bind themselves by unlawful oaths, administered secretly by Persons concealed, who artfully deceive the ignorant and unwary,—WE, the undersigned Justices think it our duty to give this PUBLIC NOTICE and CAUTION, that all Persons may know the danger they incur by entering into such Societies.

ANY PERSON who shall become a Member of such a Society, or take any Oath, or assent to any Test or Declaration not authorized by Law—

Any Person who shall administer, or be present at, or consenting to the administering or taking any Unlawful Oath, or who shall cause such Oath to be administered, although not actually present at the time—

Any Person who shall not reveal or discover any Illegal Oath which may have been administered, or any Illegal Act done or to be done—

Any Person who shall induce, or endeavour to persuade any other Person to become a Member of such Societies, WILL BECOME

# Guilty of Felony,
## AND BE LIABLE TO BE
# Transported for Seven Years.

ANY PERSON who shall be compelled to take such an Oath, unless he shall declare the same within four days, together with the whole of what he shall know touching the same, will be liable to the same Penalty.

Any Person who shall directly or indirectly maintain correspondence or intercourse with such Society, will be deemed Guilty of an Unlawful Combination and Confederacy, and on Conviction before one Justice, on the Oath of one Witness, be liable to a Penalty of TWENTY POUNDS, or to be committed to the Common Gaol or House of Correction, for THREE CALENDAR MONTHS; or if proceeded against by Indictment, may be CONVICTED OF FELONY, and be TRANSPORTED FOR SEVEN YEARS.

Any Person who shall knowingly permit any Meeting of any such Society to be held in any House, Building, or other Place, shall for the first offence be liable to the Penalty of FIVE POUNDS; and for every other offence committed after Conviction, be deemed Guilty of such Unlawful Combination and Confederacy, and on Conviction before one Justice, on the Oath of one Witness, be liable to a Penalty of TWENTY POUNDS, or to Commitment to the Common Gaol or House of Correction, FOR THREE CALENDAR MONTHS; or if proceeded against by Indictment may be

# CONVICTED OF FELONY,
# And Transported for SEVEN YEARS.

| COUNTY OF DORSET, | C. B. WOLLASTON, | HENRY FRAMPTON, |
| Dorchester Division. | JAMES FRAMPTON, | RICHD. TUCKER STEWARD, |
| | WILLIAM ENGLAND, | WILLIAM R. CHURCHILL, |
| February 22d. 1834. | THOS. DADE, | AUGUSTUS FOSTER. |
| | JNO. MORTON COLSON, | |

G. CLARK, PRINTER, CORNHILL, DORCHESTER.

18. Tolpuddle warning notice

19. James Frampton of Moreton

## Lunatic asylums in the county 1774–1850

There were more insane paupers than room for them in the hospital, where the 'dormitories were crowded beyond what is deemed right'. Again and again more rooms had to be added. Official planning was ever thus.

Under the 1845 Act the Lunacy Commissioners were empowered to inspect not only private and public madhouses but workhouses in which the insane were lodged. During 1848–9 they visited Blandford, where there were six lunatics, Cerne Abbas three, Poole four, Wareham two, Weymouth eight and Wimborne four, in addition to Forston, Halstock and Cranborne. Their energy was amazing, and to them and the county magistrates can be credited many of the improvements in the care of the insane to which the Forston records bear witness.

# CHAPTER TEN

## Some glimpses of Bridport society

At the backs of sixteen little red leather-bound volumes of *The Lady's Polite Remembrancer*, and across the spaces for daily entries, Maria Carter of Bridport kept a record of her life between 1818 and 1834. Maria was the second daughter of Joshua Carter, currier and wool stapler. The Carters were related to several local families, chief among them the Colfoxes and the Barretts. From Maria's diary it is possible to see Bridport life through the eyes of a girl in her early twenties. It was a circumscribed existence in which every visit exchanged, every letter written or received, was thought worthy of mention. Visits were made daily, even before breakfast, throughout the day and after supper. Maria even noted whom she met in the street. She knew the Gundrys, ropemakers, well. The town clerk's family, the local auctioneer, the bookseller, one of the doctors, two milliners and a dressmaker were all among her acquaintances. The Carters had been curriers for three generations at least. John, her grandfather, died in 1787 leaving his freehold toft or homestead and lands on the south side of West Street, whereon his dwelling had recently been burnt down, in trust for his son. He also had a dwelling-house next door which he held on lease from Bridport Corporation. A third property was inhabited by William, another of Maria's uncles, who was a grocer and tallow chandler. Thomas Carter, another uncle, lived at Beaminster and was also a wool currier. Joshua, Maria's father, was granted probate of the will as befitting the eldest son. He began to rebuild his father's house a few years later, employing James Hamilton of Weymouth, architect, to prepare plans for a good and substantial dwelling-house for which he agreed to pay over £600. Maria was living on the south side of West Street when the diaries opened; she later moved to East Street, and when her parents' money failed their furniture was stored and they moved to a cottage elsewhere.

## Some glimpses of Bridport society

Death and illness plays a large part in Maria's diaries. Her eldest brother only lived two days; Charles, a second brother, a bare four months; Henry only a month and Harriet scarcely longer. When Maria began to recount her daily existence both parents were living, a sister Elizabeth and a brother James. Mrs Carter was ailing. After a lingering illness she had fits, breathed very loud, so it seemed to the daughter who was sitting by her, and just as the clock began to strike eleven she died. Four days later, 'Papa, sister and self saw her dear remains deposited in the cold grave' at Netherbury. Four years later Elizabeth, who also had long been in poor health, became really ill. She was bled on two successive days, leeches were put on her chest and she was warned of her danger. 'She bore it', either the bleeding or the news, Maria is not precise, 'remarkably well and settled her affairs. We sent for the Reverend D. Williams who read prayers.' The doctor visited four times. Two days later Elizabeth died at a quarter past eleven. Joshua was to die suddenly, falling down in a fit in South Street when returning from London. He only managed to say 'Oh' before he expired. He was brought home and put, curiously, into the cellar until the funeral. No wonder Maria was often depressed; 'Spirits very bad', she wrote again and again. The health of her friends and her own were most important to her. 'Took some powders and brandy and water, being very much relaxed in my bowels.' This did not succeed, as she was immediately sick, but tincture of rhubarb seemed to help. Alarming accidents befell her friends: Mr Purchase was bitten in the leg by a dog; Mr Hearn lost his left thumb through a shooting accident; a pack of flax fell on Mr Hounsell and killed him. Mr Dowland shot himself; Mr Edwards cut his own throat. Maria herself was tossed out of a gig. No wonder her weight fell to seven stone. 'I amused myself with crying, which I often do,' she wrote on one occasion, and on another: 'I sat at home crying.' Her dreams disturbed her. After her father's death she began to dream that her brother James, too, was dead. He had left Bridport in 1820 for Poole 'where he intends to sail for Newfoundland to try his fortune'. He did not seem to succeed since he surprised the family by walking in unexpectedly nearly two years later 'very shabby from Poole'. Whatever did Maria mean by her subsequent entry 'James behaves very well'? He was off again a few months later for Mevagissey to take up a position on a ship where 'if he behaves well there is a prospect of his soon becoming captain'. Poor James, ill-luck seemed to dog his footsteps. 'We had a letter saying he had been shipwrecked. Papa wrote James and sent him a one-pound note.' Unless James were near at hand the money would not have helped very much. There is no further mention of James until a December day three years later when Maria recorded that she read over all his letters, which depressed her. At some point he had arrived at the Cape of Good Hope. Every 2 November, his birthday, Maria toasted his health in a glass of wine. It is unlikely that she ever saw him again, for her premonition came true and he died in Africa three years after her disturbing dream.

As a housekeeper Maria had various troubles. Her servant fell down in the scullery with the tea tray in her hand and broke the black tea pot, two cups, saucers and cream jugs, two white plates and the slop basin. Wisely Maria did the washing of the good china and glass herself and all the family laundry. She is pleased when there is a good drying wind for the monthly wash, which was often followed by two full days of ironing. She even got up a little after five to spray and fold the clothes before breakfast and then ironed till eight o'clock on one occasion. Spring cleaning was sometimes undertaken as late as May. But December seems an unusual month to have the parlour washed and the carpet beaten. Amid her other tasks, Maria pickled gherkins, bottled gooseberries, made gallons of elder and ginger wine and baked mince pies, lemon tarts and seed cakes. Was it economy that forced her to make an excellent pudding without eggs? She cut out her father's shirts and made some of her own dresses. Otherwise, and particularly when there was need of mourning, a sewing woman came in to help. 'Hannah Symes called. I paid her 8/6 for making stays and silk.' 'Miss Jeffery here making my pelisse.' When the Queen died Maria had to make a black frock quickly. 'Lucy here making a smock frock for me coloured sarsnet.' Later she was to win a coloured silk turban in a raffle. It is to be hoped that the colours went well together. Her father gave her a parasol too, and Miss Mirch made her a lustre gown within the month because she was going to stay with relatives at Plush and Yetminster.

Maria never mentions the household shopping, though she talks of special meals; one Christmas she enjoyed 'boiled beef and mince pies', at another goose and plum pudding. She speaks of 'an excellent boiled plum pudding' as a birthday treat and of rook pie, hare, rabbits, turkey, oysters and fowls. Pancakes for dinner must have been specially liked, for she mentions them often. Among her purchases were mourning rings and brooches, a shawl, another parasol; a friend bought two shilling tickets for her in an inn raffle for a writing-table and a tea caddy, but she was unlucky. She exchanged some old gold and silver for an eyeglass, seal and key and, prudently, the gloves and hatband sent on the occasion of a cousin's death for a morning gown; for once she was apparently not in black. 'I was out of mourning yesterday.'

We know a little of Maria's amusements. Often she played whist when visiting, and cribbage, cassino or backgammon with her father, or Pope Joan by herself. 'We played bagatelle.' 'We went to see Dr Roberts's museum.' Only her father went to the play, but she enjoyed the mummers who performed in the kitchen. She read at least two of Scott's novels, and *Jerusalem Delivered* translated from the Italian, *The Recluse of Norway* and *The Foundling of Devonshire* or *Who was She?*, a novel in five volumes by Mrs Haynes. Only once, unfortunately, did the diarist express an opinion: 'I am reading *Light and Shadows of German Life* and like it very much.' Otherwise only a title, such as *Helen's Pilgrimage to Jerusalem*, is noted.

Week by week Maria recorded what the weather was like, who preached the sermon and on what text, and even whom she sat or knelt by in chapel. 'Went to meeting to hear Reverend Atkins address the young, 29 Chapter of the 1st of Chronicles, the latter part of the fifth verse—one hour and five minutes in his sermon which was excellent.' 'Rev R. Broadley 15 Chap. of Corinthians 33 verse—a very good sermon respecting the boy that was hung yesterday at Dorchester for setting fire to a house.' She was keenly interested in the ministers and indeed secretly hoped that one of them would propose. Part of her depression came from the fact that she was still unmarried. 'I dreamt last night that I was married to Robert Hearn.' Every mood was noticed. 'Mr Warne did not shake hands with me and appeared very cool for what I cannot tell.' 'Mr Warne very friendly talked about marrying.' Unhappily Mr Warne was moved to Bristol and Maria was left to find solace in reading his sermons and in dreaming about him. She even went so far as to read the marriage ceremony over to herself and to remember how Mr Warne, on shaking hands, had said 'my hand was cold and gave it a gentle squeeze'. Mr Warne returned later to Bridport in poor health. He called frequently, though sometimes 'he neither

shook hands nor wished me a goodnight when he left'. When Mr
Carter 'threw some ink', whether accidentally or not, on one of
Maria's mops, Mr Warne gallantly tried to clean it off. He helped
Maria to wind some skeins of green silk, read poetry to her, gave
her a New Year's book, lent her his newspapers. A dream disturbed
her that he had proposed to Miss Colfox but was refused. Mr Warne
was probably suffering from consumption. 'Papa told me Mr Warne
was very ill and that he feared all was over as he had thrown up a
tea cup of blood. . . . I spent the remainder of the day crying.'
When he died, Maria hoped that she would meet him again in
heaven. His successor, Mr Teggin, introduced himself by leaving
his card with a riddle on the back. When Maria put a piece of
wedding cake under her pillow she dreamt of him. Within a year
he, too, had moved, leaving a silver thimble as a parting gift. 'I
gave him a pair of garters and he left in good spirits.' Poor Maria,
she was rarely in them herself for long. 'I heard the clock strike
every hour last night but 2, 3 and 5. I felt very nervous this morning.' It was to be hoped that she got some enjoyment from lectures
on magnetism and astronomy to which a cousin took her, or in
hearing, in 1831, a local parliamentary candidate speak. Her father
was canvassing for one of them. Perhaps it was the fever of politics
that affected Mr Carter; he became very bad-tempered. 'Papa
quarrelled with me last Saturday evening.' 'Papa cross nothing
unusual of a Sunday evening.' 'Papa went to bed last night and got
up this morning without speaking to me. He was cross because I
did not go to church.'

There are little glimpses in the diary of the political scene. Maria
mentions the polling booths, the dinner given by the successful
candidate, the fireworks and the laying by one of them, Mr War-
burton, of the first stone of the Mechanics' Institute in 1832. When
George IV was proclaimed the crowd was so great that Maria and
her sister could only see, but not hear, what was going on from
Mr Colfox's wool-loft. That same evening they returned to see 'the
procession of the late good Duke of Kent brought from Sidmouth.
The funeral pass'd the church about ½ past eight—no lights except-
ing those placed in the windows by the inhabitants—the night
being very dark. The first coach contained the Urn drawn by six
black horses, next the Hearse drawn by eight horses then followed
two mourning coaches with the Duke's travelling carriage. A
*great* concourse of people in the Town.' The coffin was placed for

the night in the church, where the Bridport Light Horse kept watch. 'The band played the dead March in Saul evening and morning.' When William IV was crowned, a crown in coloured lamps was hung up and coronation bread and beer were distributed to the poor. Once Maria saw the Grand Duke Michael of Russia pass through the town and likewise the Duchess of Clarence—'a plain woman', as also she found Princess Victoria; 'the princess is plain'.

This then was Maria Carter's life—visits to relatives, calls on friends, chapel twice every Sunday, frequent walks, collecting for the Dorcas Society, playing cards, making clothes and, when her father became poor, washing, ironing, cooking and doing without a maid. She read a little and even attempted Pope's *Essay on Man*; consulted the *Book of Fate*, heard the cuckoo and recorded her dreams. 'I dreamt I was married to Mr J. Kenway.' 'I slept with my window open last night.' 'This is the hottest summer I can remember, I took off my stays.' She visited the orangery at Abbotsbury, went to the races at Weymouth and walked the length of the Esplanade before breakfast. Her trip in a boat made her very seasick. She bathed before breakfast, too, and rode on a donkey to Chickerell. Like other women she noted when she wore her new clothes for the first time, whom she saw in the street, who had a baby, who was courting, married, sick or dead. Despite her fears for her health, Maria lived to a ripe old age, dying when she was 87.

## Bridport funerals

When Maria Carter watched the Duke of Kent's funeral cortège she commented that there were plumes only on the hearse; the horses were neither plumed nor covered; it was considered rather a shabby affair. The nineteenth century attached great importance to funerals and there was a complicated ritual, amounting to a social obligation, to see that the arrangements were correct. From the account book of the Bridport undertakers' firm of Stephens & Reynolds, who may well have known Maria, it is possible to picture the slow procession that went through the town from time to time. In 1869 Edward Gundry, aged 25, was drowned in Bridport harbour. According to the *Dorset County Chronicle*, 'the daring hardihood of Englishmen is proverbial and we have now to record the death of a young and most deserving fellow townsman . . .

through attempting to accomplish a difficult undertaking'. Apparently a shipwreck had occurred and, while inspecting it, 'Mr Gundry remarked that it would be a difficult task to touch the King Post at the pier head'. The waves were at this time of 'terrific grandeur' so that the task was a hazardous one and both Mr Gundry and a friend were drowned. Gundry was an officer in the Dorset militia, an ardent sportsman and 'almost idolised by the factory work people'. For his funeral over 150 cards were sent out and the church cushions were covered in black cloth. Even special buttons had to be made.

Seven years later Gundry's father, 'one whom all classes in Bridport have honoured and respected', died. He had been magistrate, Chairman of Sessions, Councillor and Mayor. He had promoted sanitary improvements in the town, commanded the Artillery volunteers, and had been a Provincial Grand Master of Dorset freemasons. His funeral was a walking one 'as he had lived unostentatiously and unassumingly so was he consigned to his tomb; no plumed horse, no grand trappings'. Nevertheless the funeral procession must have been a long one since the accounts mention 12 bearers, the provision of 31 pairs of gloves for ladies and 29 for men, with gloves for the tenants in addition. The hassocks were again covered in black, the bells were tolled and the long accounts even include the turnpike fees when the funeral passed to Walditch from the Hyde. For Mrs Elizabeth Gundry, the widow of Joseph of an earlier generation, the silk velvet pall had to be hired from Pratt's of Exeter for over £1. Hers must have been a magnificent funeral since 'royal bands' were provided for the officials, the mourning coach and pair was followed by two coaches with four horses, a carriage and pair for the servants and then came the private carriages. Eighteen velvet and six ordinary cloaks were needed and a dozen dinners, with ale, at £1 10s were provided. No wonder three policemen were needed too. When Miss Mary Grace Gundry died in 1863, at the age of 83, cards were sent as far as Ireland; nine bearers were hired, two helpers, and five drivers with butler, coachman and footman. No less than fourteen domestics followed in carriages.

Funeral expenses in the nineteenth century covered a multitude of articles. There were gloves to be sent to the mourners, even as far afield as Ireland, carefully selected with reference to the social class of friend or relative. There is mention of French kid, kid,

Braganza, calf, Berlin, a kind of knitted wool or cloth, with white gloves if a child were to be buried. Even the sizes of the gloves appear in some of the accounts. Bands, too, were provided for the hats, usually two yards in length, of crêpe, silk, best silk or rich silk, satin, rich ottoman, muslin or ribbon. For men of ordinary height 3½ yards of crêpe or satin, for short men 3¼ yards were provided as scarves for the pall bearers. The names of those to whom bands, scarves and gloves were to be sent all appear in the account books. The bearers were often 'professional gentlemen', augmented at times by family servants, and the carpenter, mason, plumber, butler, clerk, pew-opener, driver and ostler, beadle and sexton all figure in the accounts. On one occasion, for a military funeral, crêpe armlets were provided for the officers. The bearers and servants were sometimes provided with black suits and black epaulettes, and there were cloaks and habits for the women mourners. The usual fee for bearers was 10s 6d, drivers 5s or 7s 6d, and helpers 4s.

The cost of hiring the hearse varied with the kind: £1 1s 0d for the best hearse and pair, £3 3s 0d for a hearse and four; a coach and pair to follow was 10s 6d or £1 1s 0d, a carriage and pair 10s 6d or 7s 6d. The first mention of a motor-hearse does not come until 1918. The order of the funeral procession was carefully arranged and the undertaker noted exactly who was to travel with whom and where.

The coffins varied considerably, from £8 8s 0d for unpolished oak with elm shell to £42 10s 0d for a triple coffin of elm, oak and lead. Inside, it could be padded with flannel, quilted silk, quilted flannel and pillows, and a cambric robe might be provided. In addition feathers, plumes, and a silk and velvet pall might be hired for £11 6s 0d, white silk panels for a child and further crêpe for the carriage lamps. As well as providing the hearse with trappings, the coffin 'with furniture' and clothes for mourners, the under-taker saw to the printing of the funeral cards, printed circulars and notices in both national and local newspapers, sent telegrams and paid postage and carriage. He paid for the tolling of the church bells, and the fees to clerk, minister and registrar; cemetery fees, fees for opening the family vault and for the hire of the church bier and pall, with the services of the caretaker. In 1892 a policeman got 2s 6d and there are items for 'grave and stone' and for 'painting and lettering headstone'. Mention has been made of turnpike trust tolls and there is one occasion on which 16s 6d was spent on cleaning the road. It would appear that the undertaker was responsible only for simple entertainment. As already mentioned, in 1858, for the funeral of Elizabeth Gundry, twelve dinners and ale at £1 10s 0d were provided, presumably for the professional gentlemen. Five years later dinners still cost 2s 6d each.

On occasions the undertaker had to fetch the deceased from a distance. Miss Bools died in Weymouth in 1853, so that additional turnpike charges and refreshments were paid for. On another occasion he made arrangements for burial in Bournemouth. And there were funerals under his care bound for church, chapel, Roman Catholic and Friends burial grounds. In 1874 Alice Harris, aged 25, died from some infectious disease, since it was the undertaker who paid £1 8s 6d to the nurse, £1 10s 0d for her board, £2 5s 0d for destroying the bedding, 10s for disinfecting and 13s for stimulants, as well as undertaking the usual funeral arrangements. Afterwards he whitewashed and repainted the sickroom and the furniture in it at a charge of £1 5s 0d.

This picture of Bridport, with its emphasis on death and disaster, is possibly too gloomy. Yet the nineteenth century, with its high infant mortality rate, was perhaps more conscious of death than we are today. As Philip Hine's schoolmaster reminded the boys in a Sunday sermon, their lives were uncertain and 'perhaps the wood was already cut down that was to make their coffins and the flannel woven for the shrouds'.

# CHAPTER ELEVEN

## *Schools for the Dorset children*

Today there are several kinds of schools in the county, public schools for boys and girls, grammar and comprehensive, church and state schools. Some have a national reputation and attract children from many parts of England, others are tiny little schools, tucked away in remote villages where the children are collected by bus from the outlying farms. Some of these schools have a long history and were founded by local benefactors. Their story is the history of English education in miniature.

The oldest among the schools is in Sherborne. There may well have been a medieval foundation in the town linked with the Benedictine monastery. In 1437 the school was refounded and there was mention of a schoolmaster in Cheap Street who contributed 3s 4d to a building fund for the almshouses. References in the churchwardens' accounts of All Hallows to several schoolmasters support the theory that there must have been one grammar school at least in the town. One master seems to have been the church organist, another had a pious wife who gave an altar cloth to it. A pew was reserved for the master at a rent of 4d. When the medieval monastery was dissolved the school probably came to an end; the evidence is lacking to say with certainty that it did. In Edward VI's reign the last medieval foundations, the chantries, were dissolved. Many chantry priests had also taught. In different parts of England some of the revenue from the chantry lands was devoted to the founding of new grammar schools. The Sherborne townsfolk petitioned for such a school. In 1550 it was agreed that the town was 'a place meet and convenient for a school' and a Charter was granted. Thus the Free Grammar School of Edward VI came into being. Men of 'discretion and integrity', inhabitants of the town, were to act as governors and administer the lands granted from five dissolved chantries, the revenue of which brought in £20 13s 4d. A headmaster with a salary of £16 a year, and his undermaster at £4 were to instruct the boys in Latin. Great secrecy was to be observed by the governors in their meetings, which may have taken place in one of the rooms of the almshouses; many of the governors were almshouse brethren. Joseph Fowler, the historian of Sherborne, believes that the governors rented a schoolhouse from Sir John Horsey. This building already had a tradition, since it was earlier used by the monks as a choir school. It stood on what is today the dining-room of Sherborne School. Because the building had stood empty since 1539 it had to be repaired. This must have been unsatisfactory; complete rebuilding was undertaken at the beginning of the next century.

Perhaps because of the meagre salary the early headmasters of the school followed each other in quick succession. The governors provided a house, but this did not seem to encourage long residence. Thomas Parveys, who came from Oxford in 1562, left in the following year. Seeing that the governors had contributed to his removal costs, this seems a poor return. His successor only stayed two years. The next headmaster came and went within the year. Was it this that caused the governors to provide a cupboard, press and desk for the master's study and increase the salary? The policy succeeded, for the next master remained for eight years.

There is an interesting glimpse of Sherborne in the diary of Dr Claver Morris, a Dorset man practising in Wells. He took his boy to Sherborne to leave him in the school in 1722. The headmaster, Benjamin Wilding, was himself an old pupil of the school and to him was given a silver spoon as a kind of entrance fee. Dr Morris had to buy his son a bureau in which to keep his clothes; no longer was it a free school, for the doctor had to face £20 annual fees, with gratuities to the masters and servants at Christmas. Willie Morris had to have pens, ink and copy book, all as extras, with 7s 6d to the writing master. Willie seems to have been good-natured and, in his father's judgment, 'flexible though lazy'. For this he seems to have been whipped fourteen times until his father had to desire the headmaster to show moderation in his discipline. Dr Morris preferred that the boy should be kept in at playtime instead. Perhaps stopping his 5s regular pocket money would have been wiser. Willie seemed to have very muddy feet indeed, for it cost 6s to keep his shoes clean, but only 9d to mend his clothes.

Just about the time that Willie Morris was sent to Sherborne, John Richards of Warmwell, near Weymouth, sent his son to

Wimborne Grammar School. This, too, was a Tudor foundation. Lady Margaret Beaufort had endowed a chantry at the beginning of the sixteenth century with provision for a free grammar school 'as in the manner of Eton or Winchester'. After the dissolution the grammar school had a precarious existence until, in 1562, a new grant ensured the re-endowment of the school with much of the property of the former chantry college. This was vested in twelve substantial men of the corporation. Since the school house was in disrepair the government made a grant for refurbishing. John Walters, headmaster in 1579, was sternly rebuked by the governors and 'ordered to give better attendance unto the scholars and also to keep them in better order as well in church as in the street'. Four months later he was given notice; evidently the scholars were still rowdy. In Walters's place a Mr Hyll was chosen to be master and preacher at £30, out of which he had to pay an assistant; three rooms were set aside for school and study. Complaint arose from a later master, Giles Lawrence, that the school governors were guilty of mismanagement 'they being rural persons and of small capacity'; they refused to open letters sent to them. The headmaster accused some of them of lewd behaviour, but the master himself cannot have been above reproach; one Mary Longman 'hath used opprobrious and reproachful speech of Mr Giles Lawrence viz that he hath lived incontinently'. The governors removed the master without stating their reasons, though this was surely obvious. Under pressure 'some matters frivolous and insufficient apparently from mere malice' were brought forward. Eventually the governors were prevailed upon by the Queen's Council to reinstate the headmaster. Now battle broke out between the governors and the Council of State. It was argued that they had so far failed in their duty that the schoolhouse was in decay and the master had to teach elsewhere in the town. The matter ended with the appointment of a new headmaster who stayed only a year. He was succeeded by Mr John Geare, who in his turn left very shortly afterwards for Sherborne. There he had been elected on the recommendation of Sir Walter Raleigh and Mr Secretary Cecil. Geare's successor, William Stone, was to be involved with a case in the Court of Star Chamber.

Education at Wimborne seems to have been cheaper than at Sherborne. John Richard's fees and board were only £12 a year. On the other hand two silver spoons were necessary at entrance.

In his school outfit were twelve muslin neckcloths and five night-caps. What did he wear when he, together with his fellow scholars, attended the Shrove Tuesday cock fight at the school? Here the boys' names were drawn out of a hat and their cocks fought a knock-out tournament until only one bird remained alive. His owner, the 'Victor', enjoyed the privilege of never being whipped during Lent. He could also help a friend by clapping his hat on his posterior and saving him from the lash.

When the Brougham Commissioners enquired into charitable foundations in the early nineteenth century they commented on the 'respectable and commodious' school building—a very good schoolroom, garden and playground recently acquired. There were twenty-five day boys and fifteen boarders all being taught the classics 'but not exclusively'. For instruction in reading, writing and geography 10s 6d a quarter was charged. The fees were £2 0s 0d a term. Unlike early headmasters, the Commissioners met one who had already been at the Wimborne school for twenty years at a salary of £38.

Dorchester also had a grammar school of Tudor foundation. In 1579 Thomas Hardye of Frampton left land in Dorset, the revenues from which were to support a school established in the town ten years earlier. He willed that a learned man should be appointed, with an assistant, 'for the necessary instruction and education of children of all degrees in good discipline'. The Dorchester head-master's salary was much the same as his colleagues' elsewhere in the county. He could take dayboys and boarders. The Rector of St Peters, who was appointed in 1580, had thirty-two boys in his school. An energetic successor, Mr Robert Cheek, did much to rebuild the school in 1618. He also encouraged dramatic work, a tradition which still lasts. One of the trustees of the school, William Whiteway, noted in his diary that Mr Cheek's scholars acted two comedies in the shire hall in 1623 to entertain a visiting bishop. In between grammar, Latin and acting, a scrivener attended 'to teach such a number of scholars as are willing to learn to write, one hour every day in the week except Saturday'.

Like the governors of other schools, the trustees at Dorchester had their problems in finding suitable headmasters. Politics may have clouded the issue when in 1650 the headmaster was removed 'for want of care to preserve the repute of the school'. The usher, too, was warned to go 'as unfit by reason of his late offensive carriage'. So that the new appointment should be a success, two of the trustees were sent to Hertfordshire to pick up a personal report on a Mr Kemp. Evidently the reports were satisfactory; Mr Kemp was invited to come to Dorchester and '£50 a year, a fair house and garden, a spacious school and a public library annexed all under one roof' were offered to him. Mr Kemp declined the offer and was not even tempted by an offer of repairs to school and schoolhouse. Two months later a visit was made to Salisbury for more confidential reports. Four other names were considered in quick succession until Mr Crumlum or Crumleholme was elected. He was submaster at St Paul's and the trustees generously agreed to pay for the carriage of his books from London. All was not yet settled, because the widow of a former master had installed herself in the schoolhouse and had to be ejected. Six years later Mr Crumleholme went back to St Paul's as High Master and the search had to begin all over again. Shortly after Anthony Withers was appointed there was a chance that he might be chosen for a post at Winchester and the trustees brought pressure on him to prevent his standing.

Towards the end of the seventeenth century there seems to have been a small war of town against gown in Dorchester. The grammar school was disturbed by town boys knocking at the school door and throwing stones into the building itself. The town council sent for six of the culprits who confessed their faults and, having promised not to misbehave in this way again, were forgiven. It is to be hoped that the schoolmaster had peace. Perhaps the position of the school in the heart of the town in South Street was not an ideal one. Like the other Dorset schools, Dorchester's had largely changed its character when visited by the Commissioners in the nineteenth century. All paid £3 a year for teaching on the Eton course in the classics, 10s 6d a quarter for writing and accounts and another guinea for instruction in English. The number of boys in the school was under a dozen. Later it was to be refounded and to flourish.

In contrast with Dorchester was a little school at Broadwindsor on the edge of the county. In 1725 Robert Smith left money in his will to convert his dwelling, New House, into a school and home for a master wherein he was to teach thirteen poor boys English, Latin, Greek and Hebrew, and all this for £13 a year. Within a century this interesting curriculum had been narrowed to English, reading, writing, arithmetic and the Church catechism. There were the original number of scholars who had to provide their own books and stationery, and a like number who paid 10s 6d a quarter. The master told the Commissioners that there had been no requests ever made for instruction in classics or Hebrew. The school was to horrify the Newcastle Commissioners in mid-century when they found a school room '7 feet high, flagged with stones worn and uneven; in some places the bare ground was visible, the walls were green with damp, the fireplace ruinous, the desks old and mangled'. So low had Broadwindsor grammar school fallen. It was later closed and the endowment used elsewhere.

At Evershot another little grammar school degenerated in like manner. It began as a free school for the teaching of Latin, reading, writing and grammar, endowed by Christopher Stickland in 1628. An 'honest painful and sufficient learned schoolmaster' was to be found to teach not only the boys of Evershot, but some from Frome St Quinton. They were to acquire 'good learning, true religion and the fear of God' and stay at school till eighteen or 'unto such time as they shall be fit and able to be placed abroad at the Universities of Oxford or Cambridge or elsewhere'. Surely an ambitious project. When Brougham's Commissioners reported on Evershot school they found the buildings in good repair but the master living elsewhere, as he was the curate and had let part of the schoolhouse. Neither Latin nor any other of the higher branches of education was taught. The scholars in general being the children of artisans, small tradesmen and agricultural labourers, were removed at an early age from school. After the Christmas holidays every year they brought the master a shilling or some other trifling present, with a penny a week for pens and ink. No child under eight was admitted and then he must be able to read a chapter from the New Testament. Evershot grammar school was now no longer ambitious.

Far older than Evershot, but resembling it in many ways, was the school at Netherbury. The Brougham Commissioners were unable to trace its foundation. A survey of 1546 speaks of a grammar school endowed with £5 6s 8d. An award twenty years later came from Sir John Tregonwell out of profits from land, 'to the use of a schoolmaster to teach grammar and such other uses as should be thought most fit, meet and beneficial'. By the nineteenth century Netherbury, like Evershot, had lost its classics. 'The Latin language has not been taught within the last five years.' There were few boys at school, since there was 'a disinclination on the part of the superior orders to suffer their children to associate with those of the farming class'. Fine snobbery this. Moreover, the agricultural labourers needed their children to help on the land. In the winter thirty boys might be at school, in summer only twenty. The master, who had been there a quarter of a century, tried to swell the numbers by taking private pupils, although he had none when the visitors came. Perhaps there were none able to pass the entrance reading test from the Bible. As the master enjoyed a new house and a school room big enough to take sixty children, he must have had a leisured life.

Gillingham has a grammar school founded in Henry VIII's reign; it was thus one of the oldest in the county. Certain lands and tenements were made into a trust so that 'out of the issues and profits thereof there might be perpetually maintained a schoolmaster, for instruction of youth in good literature, for the better discharge of their duty to God, the King and the Commonwealth'. The trustees failed in their duty until a suit was brought in Chancery from which stemmed an order for new trustee regulations. At an annual meeting to which the trustees were summoned, at least in later times, by the church bell, the accounts were passed. Dinner followed at the Phoenix Inn. Once at least the school remained true to its duty to the King. During the seventeenth century the school was full of the sons of loyal gentlemen, among them Edward Clarendon, later historian of the Civil War, Lord Chancellor of England and Charles I's trusty adviser. For the times the school was large, with a hundred or so boys attending. The headmaster during the most troubled period was Robert Frampton, a staunch Royalist, who actually came to blows in public with a local tailor risen to quartermaster's rank in the Parliamentary army. Mr Frampton 'repaid with interest' the insults levied at him. Smarting under his defeat the quartermaster then ordered the schoolmaster to appear before him. Again words were exchanged and the soldier seized a pint pot to fling at his opponent, but Frampton 'would not give him time to discharge, but turned his heels higher than his head and beat him out of doors'. Next the soldier arranged to kidnap the master, and again a struggle broke out which raged through the streets until a friend intervened. Contrary to the practice of the times, Frampton was not in holy orders, but shortly after his public brawls he was ordained. This in itself was an act of courage during the Interregnum. From the pulpit he denounced the King's enemies. Fearing that he would not be allowed to remain long at liberty, his friends persuaded the teacher to resign his mastership and to withdraw to the comparative seclusion of a domestic chaplaincy. Frampton later became Bishop of Gloucester, where he continued his vigorous contributions to politics, being one of the bishops to protest against James II's Declaration of Indulgence. He refused to take an oath of allegiance to William III and was deprived of his see.

Another headmaster of Gillingham attracted notoriety by threatening any who should send their sons to a rival school established by the curate. Like many another school, Gillingham decayed somewhat. When visited by Commissioners in the nineteenth century there might be twenty little boys to be taught reading and twenty-five to be instructed in reading, writing and accounts. In fact the master and his assistant were teaching thirty paying scholars; the free grammar school had disappeared.

Another school to disappear, but for quite different reasons, was that at Milton Abbas. After the dissolution of the Abbey some of the profits from a farm in trust were used to found a free grammar school. In 1785 the Earl of Dorchester objected to a school within thirty-seven yards of his mansion. His high garden wall abutted on the school which gave 'insufficient outlet for the exercise of the schools'. It is not unreasonable to suppose that the boys may have got over the wall on occasions. The scholars, sixty or seventy of them, had come from the principal farming families and from the neighbouring gentry. Many of them boarded. The situation had not been improved by the character of the master, 'careless of his duty and of ordinary decorum'. Possibly because he was poor 'he permitted the buildings to be reduced to a state which would not permit the reception of scholars'. He used the school flooring and door jambs for fuel and thus gave support to the Earl's argument that a good house in Blandford with a large playground would be far more suitable. With the removal of the school there was no provision for education for the children of Milton Abbas unless their fathers could afford to board them in Blandford. The numbers in the town school fell to eighteen, of which two were the sons of the master; they were taught reading, writing and the classics. A few dayboys joined them, but the original parish scholars had disappeared.

By the nineteenth century the distinction between grammar schools of ancient foundation and other charitable endowments for the education of the poor was blurred. All over the country were other schools such as Yetminster, founded by the scientist Robert Boyle in 1717, where twenty boys were to be taught without payment reading, writing and the casting of accounts. Shaftesbury had a school founded a year later for twenty boys and girls for instruction in the three R's and the principles of Christianity. They were to be given yearly a complete suit of outer clothing with hat and shoes, were to attend Sunday service and receive a Bible and prayer book on admission at the age of ten. At thirteen they were to be given a dark blue suit and apprenticed with a premium paid from the charity. At Lytton Cheney boys between six and fifteen were to be taught the three R's and grammar in a spacious hall and large classroom. In Melbury Osmund Mrs Susanna Strangways Horner, as mentioned in Chapter Five, gave money in 1754 for the education of twenty poor children. She further helped Abbotsbury, where in addition to the three R's the art of navigation was included 'to render them fit for sea service'. At Corfe Mullen, Lockyer's foundation of 1730 provided for thirty boys and girls to be taught by a discreet woman, a spinster without children. She had to undertake to glaze the schoolhouse windows at her own expense, though the trustees were to look after the hedges and ditches. After the Whit Monday service mistress and pupils were to be examined by the trustees in the catechism. As a reward each child was to receive a penny loaf, the girls were to get a frock and the boys a smock frock. After the inspection the trustees could eat a five-shilling dinner. The schoolmistress had to be discreet but not necessarily learned, since she had only to teach reading and needlework for which each pupil paid twopence a week. Much the same provisions governed the Charity at Sturminster Marshall, where boys up to the age of thirteen and girls to fifteen were instructed in reading, knitting and the catechism. If any boys should be wanted to drive the plough at any season before they were thirteen they should be excused school. At Easter a penny cake and a sixpenny loaf were distributed. For a time the master taught in his own house till the lord of the manor gave land for a school. Occasionally boys were taught in the evening when they were working during the day. All children left school equipped with a Bible and prayer book.

Evening schools were to be found in several parts of the county, at Marnhull and Preston for example. At Corfe Mullen the mistress had to be a single woman, at Gillingham's foundation in Wimborne the master must be single or a widower. Was a wife feared as a distraction? At Nether Compton Charity School reading, writing, spinning, knitting and sewing were offered for a penny a week. Here the move to provide education was made through Thomas Thompson, a Quaker, who ran a boarding school in the district. He gave the schoolhouse and was supported in the foundation 'by several charitable persons who have been educated at the boarding school'. Another Quaker, Daniel Taylor, benefited Bridport. From the rents of the Bull Inn, which curiously he appeared to own, an honest and discreet person, skilful and experienced in the art of reading, writing and arithmetic was to instruct thirty or so children. If the master at any time proved to be an ill-liver or guilty of any immorality or misbehaviour or ignorance, the trustees could remove him. Bere Regis, Weymouth, Wareham, Poole, Dorchester, to mention only a few other places, all had small charitable foundations for education. Hampreston had none, though the vicar sorely wanted a day school. 'The parishioners are chiefly poor but formerly prosperous when smuggling was more in practice', was the report to the Brougham Commission:

> It is a most wretched place, the principles of morality of the major part are so contaminated with smuggling that it is despaired of reclaiming them although the rector gives double duty and has not ceased to warn the inhabitants of their danger both in private and in public. If a good day school could be established in the parish it would be attended with the most salutary effects.

In the early years of the nineteenth century a Select Committee made an exhaustive enquiry into the provisions that existed for the education of the poor. Every parish was asked what endowments existed for schooling, what other schools were established there and if there were sufficient educational facilities. In Dorset there were twenty-nine parishes without either a Sunday school, a dame school or a charitable institution. The two newly founded societies, the National Society and the Lancastrian or British and Foreign Society had opened a number of schools. The schools of the former Church of England Society were in the majority, only in a few places like Poole and Blandford were there nonconformist schools. Many landowners, among them the Earl of Shaftesbury, Lady Caroline Damer and William Morton Pitt gave active support. Sometimes the vicar alone maintained the school or had the power of nomination. In some instances the bailiff, the corporation or the lord of the manor said who should be educated. Nevertheless, there were insufficient school places. In parish after parish comes the observation—the poor are desirous of having greater means. The vicar of Buckland Newton was of the opinion that 'the desire for education is daily increasing throughout the country'. Nevertheless the need for child labour in the fields was an obstacle. At Chardstock it was stated that parents were not able to spare their children from the fields or many more would attend. 'I am afraid your farmers are like farmers elsewhere. Having little or no education themselves they are very jealous of any instruction that is offered to the labouring classes whom they fear will tread on their heels.' At Pentridge, when the Earl of Shaftesbury and the rector supported a Sunday school it was said that 'no other school would answer any good purpose as all the boys and most of the girls are employed in husbandry as soon as they are able to work'. In Bradpole 'the town trade interferes but perhaps an evening school would be useful'. Sometimes poverty was felt. 'The poor [of Chalbury] can ill afford and would be extremely thankful for assistance.' Extreme poverty was mentioned for Lillington. In Portland the quarrymen, it was said, were only paid once a year and therefore had to live on credit, paying higher than market prices for their flour, and thus could not spare money for schooling. The farmers were sometimes hostile, even in one parish to a Sunday school. At Kimmeridge and Marnhull it was observed that parents did not avail themselves of what existed, but this was exceptional.

More Sunday schools existed than day schools and there were also evening schools, a private classical academy kept, curiously, by a woman, a classical and commercial academy and very many little dame schools. The description of some of the teachers is unflattering. Lydlinch suffered from a negligent master, West Parling had an elderly female, Preston had three poor women as dames. 'It is but little they pays me and it is but little I teaches them,' must have been true in many villages. To keep the children out of mischief was possibly as much as could be achieved. There is a modern note in the return from Piddlehinton: 'More could be admitted to the Sunday school if the room were larger.' At Preston the vicar had to abandon his Sunday school for want of a room; it is a pity that the return does not state why the parents at Winterbourne Abbas were 'dissatisfied with the progress of their children'.

In the schools supported by the National Society, whether day or Sunday schools, teaching by the Madras system was employed. This system of instruction by monitors had been developed by Dr Bell, who was rector of Swanage in 1801. He had earlier served as Superintendent of the Madras Orphan Asylum in India, where he had created the system of child teaching which was to be largely employed in England and much praised for its cheapness. When Dr Lancaster instituted his Nonconformist Educational Society he acknowledged his indebtedness to Bell, with whom he stayed in Swanage for a few days. Among Dr Bell's helpers at the Swanage school was Lewis Warren, a Sunday school teacher. When he was thirteen he was sent to Whitechapel to introduce the monitorial system. The chairman of the school thanked Dr Bell for 'sending so promptly that interesting and intelligent lad'. Lewis, however, found trouble in controlling these London children. A visitor to the school commented on the noise. Dr Bell had to come up to town to set things right and persuade the schoolmaster to support Lewis. Success was now achieved. 'The boys' Sunday school has made so good progress on Dr Bell's plan as to give me the greatest pleasure, and to enable me to show it to many people as a fair specimen of the excellence of the system.' 'I have pleasure in stating that the children here . . . seem to be rapidly improving . . . our little instructor seems very well calculated for his office; he carries authority with him, and makes boys twice his size stand in awe of him, but out of school is as much a child as any of them.' Others now wanted Dr Bell's teachers. Dr Andrews . . . wants a Lewis Warren (or, if it could be, one looking more like a master) for the school at St James'. Warren seems to have been hard-worked, since he was used in a day school and two Sunday schools. Two years later he was sent to the West Indies to introduce Bell's methods. The planters, however, did not welcome him and the attempt ended in failure.

The first branch of the National Society for the Education of the

Poor in the Principles of the Established Church was founded in Dorset in 1812, some years after Bell had gone to Swanage. The county was divided into nine areas with the energetic Morton Pitt as President, supported by many leading figures who subscribed to the funds. Grants from the Society were applied for and the first Society school was opened at Buckland Newton in 1816. In the next twenty years thirteen more schools came into existence and many of the older charity schools were merged with a transference of funds. Some money came from the Society to help with building, but local people had to raise funds by the time-honoured method of arranging bazaars. At Buckland Newton the landowners agreed to a shilling in the pound voluntary rate to support the teacher. He was luckier than one at Spettisbury, where there was a charity foundation. Thomas Harvey, the master, wrote to one of the trustees in 1816 that he had so few scholars, no salary and, being faced with rising prices, was forced to borrow £100. The trustee was sympathetic, 'I shall be ready to advance part of the £100. When it is recollected that the salary is small and from the sad arrangement of the finances of the school . . . I do not think his request unreasonable.'

A subsequent letter to the vicar said that 'the other trustees have not considered themselves justified in assisting him but trust we shall all act equally for the benefit of the school'. Surely to have paid the master would have helped the school?

As the nineteenth century advanced money was available from the Salisbury Diocesan Board for some schools and Treasury grants were made to certain parishes; Rampisham got £15, Ibberton £25 provided the final building plans were approved and inspection accepted. The church grants, too, were conditional on inspection, which was not always welcome. At Lyme Regis 'the word inspection does not include the examination of our scholars, neither shall they open their lips in the schoolroom so as to interfere with the Rules. If such an attempt is made I shall instantly dismiss the school and the inspectors may seek their remedy where they can.' But stronger still was the comment in the Netherbury school records: 'Down with the church, down with it even to the ground.' Schoolrooms were improvised in cottages, workhouses, inns and in the church or parsonage—temporary expedients which have been resorted to again in our time.

When the Brougham Commissioners enquired into Dorset

education there were 48 charity schools, 147 Sunday schools, 126 dame schools, with a number of day schools, either National Society, Lancastrian, Congregational, Methodist or Baptist, in addition to the evening, private and grammar schools. The Sunday schools had far longer sessions than today. A printed form among the county archives shows that at Bridport Sunday school began at 9 am with the register and prayers. A second session opened at two in the afternoon and ended at five in winter, six in summer. There were three classes. Details had to be entered of absence with the cause; bad behaviour, withdrawal or expulsion. If admonitions were sent to parents they had to be noted; also which pupils received Bibles, prayer books or spellers, and which children could not attend because they had no clothes. There seems to have been a system of rewards of a halfpenny or a penny and there were cakes too. The teachers were paid sixpence a week. Between January 1793 and May 1794, 408 children were admitted and 196 left, the number on roll in 1794 being 212. If there were only three classrooms the modern teacher has nothing to complain of in comparison. To meet the costs of running the school certain townsfolk subscribed and there were church collections. Other Sunday schools were run entirely at the expense of the minister, as at Bincombe where twenty-four children attended. At Chalbury it was the curate who bore the charge. At Gillingham 'the middling class of people have undertaken the office of teachers' at the voluntary Sunday school. At Okeford Fitzpaine the Sunday school had the support of the Society for the Propagation of Christian Knowledge. Generally speaking the monitorial system was used in the Sunday schools as in the day schools.

Of the hundred or so dame schools few records exist. They were usually small and often short-lived. There were twelve in Weymouth in 1818, Puddletown had six and tiny Long Burton five. The words of one dame, 'If I can keep a bit of quietness it is as much as I can do and as much as I am paid for,' must have been true of many. To teach a little reading was as much as they attemped. At Maiden Newton they 'generally teach nothing or to read in a sing-song tone which has to be unlearnt. The schools are more to take care of the children.'

The genteel private schools for the upper classes were little better. Elizabeth Ham has left us a picture of her Weymouth schools as at the end of the eighteenth century. She went first to one kept by 'a little old widow lady . . . here I learnt nothing but reading spelling and sewing'. She remembered with pleasure the day floods covered the town near the Quay where the school was situated. Later it moved to St Mary's Street, near the Esplanade, where Elizabeth was now a weekly boarder. She writes with anguish of the hours spent 'with hot hands and creaking needle . . . in a closed room, packed side by side on a long form with others as hot and sleepy as myself'. 'A shirt was a weary long while in hand . . . my work was slow and dirty and not at all satisfactory to my Mamma.' Mrs Ham took her daughter back to school in person one Monday to complain and was curtly informed that 'she was at full liberty to remove her daughter as soon as she liked'. This Mrs Ham did immediately, and another school was selected. Of her schoolmistresses Elizabeth said sadly: 'not one of the governesses it was my fate to be placed under knew as much education as could now be found in any mistress of any village charity school'. Dreary indeed must the evenings have been when *Pilgrim's Progress* was read night after night. Of another school, in Devonshire, but probably just as true of Dorset, Elizabeth said:

> We learned by rote either from the dictionary, the grammar or geography. We wrote no exercises nor were we asked any questions about our lessons. We read from the Bible in the morning and the History of England or Rome in the afternoon. A master came to teach us writing and cyphering from 11–12 and a dancing master once a week.

Shortly after Elizabeth moved from school to school Philip Hine went to Blandford Academy where he began Latin grammar before breakfast, which was at eight o'clock, immediately preceded by family prayers. At nine-fifteen school began again with Caesar and Virgil. After the midday meal at twelve, Philip walked or played rounders until two. A history lesson and some cyphering had to be fitted in before six o'clock when probably he had tea. A game of ball followed, after which he returned to study his lessons and write his exercise and his journal. His studies at Blandford seem wider than was usual in 1825, since his diary mentions chemistry and geography. A whole morning could be spent parsing. On Sunday he had to listen to upwards of four sermons, learn his catechism and read an improving magazine. He did however read *Robinson Crusoe* some time during his school days.

# Schools for the Dorset children

*Some Dorset record books 1860–1880: a postscript*

Week after week during the school term, headmistresses and masters entered special events in their school record books and from these books a picture emerges of Dorset children which has its charm and its interest. The following details have been drawn from five log books, three of them of schools now closed and two where the schools still flourish.[1]

The schools themselves were not large; where details are given it would appear that there were 76 children on the Shapwick roll and 130 on the Sturminster, with 84 at Wool, but numbers fluctuated.

This was a time when education was neither free nor, until after 1881, compulsory. The school fees varied—at Shapwick and Sturminster a penny a week was charged, which in 1875 was raised to twopence. Wool charged three-halfpence, and double fees if the luckless pupil failed the annual inspectorial examination. Children were admitted at any age from five to twelve and they came and went almost at will. Time and time again the schoolmistress bewailed their irregular attendances: 'Progress not satisfactory as the parents do not value education and do not send their children.' They were kept away potato-picking, haymaking or bird-scaring; there were village fairs and other attractions such as sales, funerals, 'temperance feasts' or 'methodist teas'. Then there were the children who played truant. On one occasion the Sturminster pupil-teacher set out in pursuit of two boys, but she could only catch one miscreant, the other ran too fast for her. Of course, illness kept children away—there is mention of chicken-pox, whooping cough, mumps, measles, ringworm and, in July 1864, smallpox was raging at Sturminster.

When the children did attend, they were instructed by a mistress with the help of a pupil-teacher and possibly, in the larger schools, a monitor. One is struck by the frequent changes in the staff. Between 1864 and 1880 at Wool there were ten changes of teacher. This may have been due to the heavy burden of numbers, since the teacher was not only responsible for the eighty-four or so children, but had also to instruct the pupil-teacher, often from six-thirty to eight in the morning before school began. And the pupil-teachers, hardly more than children themselves, must often have been a sore trial. 'Reprimanded the pupil-teachers for care-

[1] The schools are Pentridge, population in 1861—295; Shapwick—446; Woodsford—193; Wool—590 and Sturminster Newton—1880.

lessness in their lessons.' Though at another time the mistress could declare that she examined 'the First Standard in writing. Many of them did their capital letters very nicely. The pupil-teacher deserves great praise for her work in this matter of writing.' There were occasions when a school had to be closed because no teacher could be found. Once, at Wool, when the mistress was away the curate's sister came to the rescue, and sometimes the child monitors carried on alone. It is not surprising that in overcrowded conditions at Sturminster in 1866, where 130 children were packed into two rooms, and with irregular attendance, the children were inattentive and had to be kept in after school. They were 'very troublesome', blotted their copy books so that they had to be kept back with a lesson for bad behaviour or made to write out lines. One such girl, punished for being late, was promptly withdrawn by her parents. A boy being punished for constant unpunctuality actually jumped out of the school window. Time and again the poor schoolmistress complained of idleness, of children daring to laugh during prayers, of noise, or of talking during needlework. One can feel the utter exasperation of the Wool mistress who kept in the whole school in May 1866 for talking. The children were 'rude' and 'rough'; the boys fought, they broke the school cane, they told lies and said 'bad words'; they broke their slates, they answered back. What they learnt during term they forgot during the holidays. In January 1864, at Sturminster, sadly the teacher wrote, 'they seemingly have no desire to learn', and this was echoed bitterly at Pentridge. 'Sorry I am so sharp tongued with the children as to deserve a rebuke from the Inspector, but do not see how I can alter, as most of them are encouraged at home to be rebellious at school and therefore I am stern with them to have a little discipline or I should have mistresses instead of being mistress.' Yet the picture is not one of unrelieved gloom. There were prizes for good attendance; a generous lady at Sturminster offered a prize to the one who took most pains in her writing; later the vicar's wife gave away 'pinafores and 3 pairs of woollen cuffs to those most regular for half-a-year'. And there was a happy time when both pupil-teachers gained a prize of ten shillings each in their annual examination.

This examination was part of a system of payments by results whereby the amount of Government grant was calculated on the number of pupils who successfully attained a required standard. As all the schools were Church foundations there was, in addition, the Bishop's Inspection conducted by a local parson. For example, the ecclesiastical visit took place at Sturminster on 2 December 1863, to be followed in February by the Government Inspector, who reported that the arithmetic was very weak in the upper part of the school. One pupil, however, did so well that she was given a shilling by the Reverend Mr Lownes. Obviously the mistress was having a struggle to improve the arithmetic, for she wrote in May that 'the older girls will take no delight in it'. Her efforts must have had some effect, as the next report said that the school was doing better than last year, especially in reading and arithmetic. Despite the mistress's gloomy forecast 'nearly the whole of them are remarkably stupid and it is much to be feared will never pass the Government examination', the report of 1866 spoke of improvement in every respect. 'The mistress has worked very hard and with success.' The mistress thereupon left. In common with all incoming teachers, the new head noted that 'she found the children very backward, with arithmetic poor throughout the school'. However, the inspectors in their turn were to find defective teaching, due, they felt, to neglect on the part of the mistress, so that they recommended a reduction in the grant by a tenth. It can hardly have been chance that a new mistress appears in the next month. The inspectors interested themselves, not only with attainments, but also with equipment. 'H.M. Inspector further reports that the supply of slates was insufficient last year. I called the attention of the Managers to the fact then. This year it continued to be insufficient.' Alas, in Wool in 1872, 'the examination was most unsatisfactory. My Lords have had considerable hesitation in allowing an unreduced grant; very much better results must be shown next year.' The teacher seemed to have left in consequence and for the next few years H.M. Inspector reports harshly: 'I fear the assistance rendered by the pupil-teachers is infinitesimal and their examination papers are discreditable to themselves and their teachers.' The grant was reduced and the school was visited without notice on a number of occasions. Mistress followed mistress in quick succession and it was not until 1880 'that creditable progress could be reported'; even then the schoolroom wanted painting, and a map of England and another blackboard were needed.

Reading the notes on the work done by the children in the different schools, one is not surprised that inattention, talking, and lack of progress were mentioned. How long the day must have seemed when the whole of it was spent on needlework, and that in making waistcoats for poor children, or 'shirts, pinafores, aprons, sent to the Vicarage', or on another occasion twelve calico tea cloths, or how dreary a whole morning struggling with the 'three times' table. How the school must have rejoiced 'at the appearance of a ferret', surely a relief from writing out the names of the principal persons in the book of Genesis. Perhaps because they were far fewer, school treats were even more enjoyable then —the Prince of Wales's wedding was celebrated with a holiday and tea and cake all round. And then the vicar treated the school to the circus. There is an occasional mention of a school concert, or of school ending early because the building was needed for an evening entertainment to which the children were allowed to go.

There are a few glimpses of the outside world. Girls left Sturminster to learn gloving. The children arrived late in the afternoon 'because they have been hanging about to see the arrival of the Engine for the first time'. On one occasion in 1873 the Woodsford mistress noted '9 children left school, their fathers having joined the Labourers' Union were sent from the Parish'.

In the eighteen-eighties some broadening of the curriculum can be seen, with nature lessons on the crocodile, cat, donkey, hedgehog, cabbage, holly, oak, and the like. Poetry, too, found a place, with Standard 6 studying Gray's *Elegy*, Standard 4 *The Village Blacksmith* and the Infants *The Skylark*. One wonders if this was the reason why when 'the Diocesan Inspector wished the children to have a half-holiday, they thanked him but said they would rather come to school'. On the whole, however, in the twenty earlier years, the insistence on arithmetic, sewing, knitting, writing, Old Testament scripture with spelling, suggests that Matthew Arnold's strictures on the system of payment by results were well-founded, and there are abundant examples of 'deadness, slackness, and discouragement'. 'There is no probability of Sarah White learning weights and measures.' 'Parents must be visited and asked to insist upon the children learning their lessons.' 'It is most difficult to get the children. The boys seem employed and the girls are kept at home to do the gloomy work.' 'The schoolroom is very cold; the supply of coal exhausted.' 'The mistress will do well to put a little more energy into her teaching.' Poor mistresses, theirs was no easy lot!

# CHAPTER TWELVE

## *Industries*

U ntil the coming of the Industrial Revolution Dorset had a number of industries which depended on natural deposits, such as quarrying, or on local crops of flax and hemp with which the rope, net and sailcloth manufacture were linked. Cloth of different kinds, gloves, buttons, lace and stockings were all produced in the county. Quarrying and ropemaking were medieval in origin and are still flourishing. Other industries could not easily make the transition from cottage to factory organization.

The most important early industry was the production of Purbeck marble. Nearly every English church of any size built between the twelfth and fourteenth centuries had such stone in it. There are twelfth-century marble fonts at Martinstown, Loders and Mappowder, at St Cross in Winchester and at Battle in Sussex. The effigy of Philip the priest at Tolpuddle, Bishop Josylen de Bohun in Salisbury Cathedral and Abbot Clement in Sherborne are of Purbeck stone. In the next century marble left the county in great quantities. A letter from King John to the bailiffs of the Dorset seaports says that licence had been given to the Bishop of Chichester to carry away his marble from Purbeck to Chichester. The bailiffs must allow him to do so, having taken security that it goes nowhere else. The effigy of the King himself in Worcester Cathedral is of this marble. The development of the Early English Gothic style with its polished shafting rising round a central column encouraged the extensive use of Dorset marble. From the quarries of Peter and William de Clavile came stone for Westminster Abbey. The sheriff's accounts speak of one shipload of marble to the Tower of London and four loads of Purbeck at £30 16s 4d. Nicholas Red and his fellow surveyors were paid £35 for 'marble at Purbeck for the King's works at Westminster'. 'I am sending you the shipload of marble by William Justice whom you may pay for freight 5½ marks and 10 shillings and if God prosper us I will send you a ship load before Whit Sunday and a third if I can find a ship to carry the said stone,' wrote Robert de Bremele from Purbeck. Another letter from Richard le Wyte, of the quarry at Purbeck, assures Robert de Beverley that he has hurried on with the quarrying for the King. To Tarrant Monkton went a carved effigy to adorn the tomb of the Queen of Scotland for 100 shillings. Not only did marble go from Purbeck, but master masons went to settle in London. They must have worked at Westminster and perhaps on the Purbeck marble columns of the round Temple Church, where four knights are carved in chain mail out of Dorset stone. Henry III was entombed in Purbeck marble, as were Edward I and the Black Prince. Some of the crosses which marked the resting-places of the coffin of Queen Eleanor of Castile came from Purbeck. 'To Robert de Corfe in part payment for three shafts, three heads, three rings of marble for crosses at Lincoln, Northampton and Waltham 5 marks. To Edward of Corfe for 1300½ stone and freight £5 3s 4d. To Robert de Corfe 55 yards of stone and freight £4 17s 6d' appear in Edward I's accounts. This would suggest that the stone was sent rough-hewn or partly carved. Edward I had also to pay for a marble altar which his father had given to the Friars of Mount Carmel.

Exeter, Salisbury, Ely, Wells and Worcester have Purbeck marble shafts. The string courses and shafts at Chichester are of this stone. William de Sens used it in his new choir at Canterbury. Fonts, effigies and piscinas were made at Corfe, where a school of local sculptors polished the marble and executed the commissions for capitals, bases and other mouldings. Modern building excavations in Corfe have revealed masons' rubbish, pieces of dressed marble and fragments of moulding and ornaments many feet deep in parts of West Street.

Among the Dorset masons who settled in London was Adam de Corfe to whom 50s was paid for a slab to place on the high table of the king's palace at Westminster. Later he provided paving for St Paul's. Adam lived in Farringdon Ward in the City and died in 1331, leaving a tenement in East Street, Corfe. Almost contemporary with him was Henry Yevele, one of the few medieval architects known by name. He worked in Westminster Abbey, Canterbury and old St Paul's, on the Tower and on London Bridge among other places. Yevele also executed commissions for non-royal patrons. A warrant of 1374 addressed to the keepers of the port of Poole ordered them to release from arrest the ship *Margarete* of Wareham of forty-eight tons burthen, with two high tombs of marble for the Earl of Arundel and Eleanor his late wife, one great stone for the Bishop of Winchester, and other things of theirs which were on board. The ship had been seized for an expedition to France. It was to be taken to London and there unloaded, Master Henry Yevele, mason, being the principal surety. The Earl and his wife were buried in Lewes Priory; their effigies were moved to Chichester Cathedral after the dissolution. When John of Gaunt returned to England after his disastrous French campaign he began extensive building at Kenilworth Castle, where Yevele was employed. The mason was subsequently granted wardship of the manor of Langton Matravers in Purbeck until the coming of age of Joan, heiress of John le Walsh. This no doubt strengthened Yevele's interest in the quarries. The fact that Purbeck marble was used by him for the tomb of the Black Prince in the year of the grant suggests that he may have supplied the marble from his own quarry.

One family of quarry-owners in Purbeck had a long history. William Canon owned property before 1288 and supplied marble for some of Queen Eleanor's crosses, among them Charing Cross. In the Exeter fabric rolls comes the item 'paid to William Canon of Corfe 1291 £26 13s 4d'. His son supplied sixty pairs of columns, bases and capitals for the cathedral at £15, twenty-nine for the cloister at £1 1s 9d and many other pieces. So satisfied were the Dean and Chapter that when the work was completed in 1354 William Canon received a bonus of £4. He was the highest-taxed citizen of Corfe and Mayor of the town. From Richard Canon came marble for Canterbury in 1337. Edmund Canon worked as a stonecutter in St Stephen's Chapel at Westminster. A later William carved angels for Westminster at 20s each and John Canon was working as a mason in 1422 at Hertford Castle.

Changes in architectural style caused a decline in the demand for Purbeck marble after 1400. There was no longer a need for polished clustered shafts. Softer freestone lent itself more easily to sculpture and effigies. Rival centres had developed in Kent, Sussex and Durham; alabaster was now more favoured, and though some alabaster was worked in Dorset the glories of the Purbeck industry declined. The tracks from the quarries to Poole harbour became grown over and are now more easily visible from the air.

# Industries

There are no medieval records extant of the organization of the Purbeck masons, but Tudor regulations are probably older than 1551. These bylaws of the Company of Marblers or Stone Cutters of the Isle of Purbeck provided for the election of two wardens and two stewards yearly at a court at the Corfe Guildhall. The wardens were to adjudge quarrels, settle disputes about encroachments, and register apprentices, who had to appear at the court with a penny loaf in one hand and a pot of ale in the other. Only the freemen could quarry. The widow of a freeman could take apprentices, who had to serve for seven years, living in their masters' homes. No one base-born might be apprenticed. On Shrove Tuesday following his marriage, the marbler must pay a fine of twelve pence and the most recently-married man must come with a football which, a later set of bylaws said, must be carried to Owrekey. The Company had a common stock in charge of the wardens. There were fines if members did not cease their chatter when silence was called for at the yearly meeting or if secrets of the Company were revealed.

At the end of the seventeenth century the Purbeck stone quarrying which had taken the place of marble was declining, due, it was said, to several dealers in stone sending it direct to London in small quantities and undercutting each other. Regulations were made in 1697 that all stone should be sold as a company joint stock managed by men of integrity and honour. When Claridge reported on the industry in 1793 he found 400 employed in quarrying stone for walling, floors, pavements and steps, with a thinner variety used for roofing. Fifty thousand tons were shipped annually from Swanage. The Corfe census, discussed elsewhere, gives the rates of pay at that period. Stone is still quarried in Purbeck.

## Portland stone

One of the most thriving industries is to be found in Portland, which sticks out into the sea, a huge block of stone, described recently as being 'like the beak of a huge bird at the end of the long neck of the Chesil ridge'. Until recently almost an island linked to the mainland by a ferry, Portland is unlike the rest of the adjoining county. Its inhabitants were, in Hardy's words, a 'curious and well-nigh distinct people cherishing strange beliefs and singular customs for the most part obsolescent'. In the past many lived by smuggling, fishing or quarrying. At a Weymouth parliamentary election in

# Industries

1826 'numerous gangs of desperate individuals, lawless bodies of smugglers and whole families of Portlanders were hired to assist in securing the introduction of voters'. The military had to be called in, but not before the Mayor had been knocked down, poll booths destroyed and the hall taken by storm.

The Portland quarries were first worked in the early Middle Ages; some stone was exported by sea to Exeter for the cathedral in the fourteenth century and to Westminster for the royal palace. Portland Castle, built in Tudor times, was of the same stone. When Leland visited Portland 'environed by the sea' he noted that there were but eighty houses on it. Ruins of others suggested a fall in the number of inhabitants. 'The people of the island live now by tillages and somewhat from fishing. They be good there in slinging of stones and use it for defence of the Island.' In 1593 Queen Elizabeth appointed a royal surveyor to the quarries.

The important development of the quarries began, however, in James I's reign. In 1619 the banqueting hall in Whitehall was burnt down. Within six months Inigo Jones was ready with designs for a new building, for which he proposed to use Portland stone. At the time the tenant of the quarries was Nicholas Jones, who may have been a relation of the architect. A new pier was built on the island from which the stone was to be sent to London. St Paul's Cathedral needed repair; £20,000 worth of stone was to come from Portland. The crane on the pier had to be repaired. A few years later the Duke of Richmond needed a thousand tons of stone for his house in Holborn and more was ordered for York House for the Duke of Buckingham.

Peter Munday has left us a picture of Portland at this time. He was impressed by the castles, the caves and the race off the Bill. There was a trade in what he called peewits, more probably black-head gulls, which were sent to London as delicacies. When he visited the island, two hundred workmen were engaged in quarrying stone for St Paul's. Great masses weighing many tons were moved on two-wheel trolleys drawn by eight horses. 'When I viewed the simple construction of their carriages I could not but wonder—a pair of very stout wheels about a yard in diameter and a very thick axle tree on which was a stout platform carrying astonishing weights of up to six tons.' These carts or trolleys were used till almost the end of the nineteenth century. When the carts were descending an incline more stone was tied behind as a brake.

# Industries

When Christopher Wren came to rebuild St Paul's Cathedral after the Fire he used Portland stone. There was considerable interference by the pressgangs with the crews of his stone-carrying ships until he gained exemption for them. He seems to have found the Portlanders troublesome, for he wrote in firm terms in 1705:

> You have been paid hitherto beforehand but without your better behaviour you shall not be paid so again though you may always depend on what is right . . . as to the stone you have sent to Greenwich I know no risk you have run, nor of any proposed to you; so that you have no pretence to higher pay on that account. 'Tis all one to me what your jury do. It shall not alter any measures of mine, except in endeavouring that the tonnage money you claim by a pretended grant from the Crown be disposed to better purpose than you apply it to, you have no manner of right to it, as I shall easily make appear . . . for although 'tis in your power to be as ungrateful as you will, yet you must not think that your insolence will always be borne with and though you will not be sensible of the advantage you receive by the present workings of the quarries yet if they were taken from you, I believe you might find the want of them in very little time.

Wren then went on to hope that only those would be employed 'as will work regularly and quietly and submit to proper and reasonable directions', which suggests that there had been trouble. This letter was addressed to six Portlanders, among them Bartholomew Comben and Henry Atwel, names still to be found on the island.

From 1675 to 1707 Wren virtually controlled the output of stone from the quarries. He approved the stone with a personal symbol, a letter Y marked on the pieces.

Portland was a royal manor, but any commoner had the right to take stone for his own use within the island. All stone taken for other use carried a royalty of twelve pence a ton payable to the lord of the manor. Before the Restoration this royalty was apportioned, a half to the lord and a half to the tenants, but Charles II 'calling to mind the constant Loyalty and Affection of the said Island to us and to our late Royal Father of ever glorious memory', remitted half the Crown's share.

By the end of the eighteenth century Claridge could note that between thirty and forty thousand tons of stone were exported annually. The owner of the land got 1s a ton and the workmen, of whom there were eight hundred men and boys got 6s for raising the stone, 2s 6d for carriage to the ships and freightage to London, 10s in peace-time and 14s during the war. There seem to have been upwards of fifty ships in this trade. Another visitor at this time speaks of the laborious business of raising the huge blocks of stone, a hundred men and more working on one piece which was afterwards broken into smaller blocks. In the past the gangs were usually composed of members of one family who provided and maintained their own tools, the quarrymaster providing such lifting tackle as was necessary. To help the men who were putting in their wedges before lifting was undertaken, the quarry leader used to chant a song to ensure that all the men struck their wedges in unison. There is a tradition that the quarry boy perched on top of the rock sang *The French Song* which lasted long enough for all the strikers to get in their wedges truly. One that came loose before the song ended had to be paid for with half a gallon of ale. The boy kept a tally of the fines—and also the traditional two-gallon stone jar—and as soon as he had recorded enough fines to fill it this was done and the jar emptied. Another custom, practised as late as 1890, was the pay-off, when a newly-married man returned to work. After a dinner a jump was arranged over a piece of wood held by the most recently-married man and the next one likely to marry. Solemn regulations were read out before the jump was made.

Although these customs have largely died out and mechanization has come to the industry, the stone still goes up to London by road for the repair of the capital's great buildings. Mouldings and sculptured pieces leave Portland for this purpose. Town halls, shops, bridges, offices and police courts all over the country bear evidence of this Dorset industry.

## Rope and net making

Quite one of the most interesting industries of the county is centred on Bridport, which was a borough at the time of the Domesday Survey. It is probable that flax and hemp were already grown in the area round about, since there are Saxon place-names connected with the crop. King John visited the town at the beginning of the thirteenth century and wrote to the Sheriff of Dorset in 1213 'we command you that as you love us . . . you cause to be made at Bridport night and day, as many ropes for ships, both large and small, as many cables as you can and twisted ropes for cordage for ballistae'. Orders had already been issued in 1211 for 1,000 yards of cloth for ships' sails and 3,000 weights of hempen thread for ships' cables at a cost of £48 9s 7d. Thus began the link between Bridport and the King's ships which was to last through the centuries. The industry grew steadily in the Middle Ages. Ropers from Bridport established a new industry at Newcastle. The Bridport town documents bear evidence of trade with London and Portsmouth. The Hundred Years War with France meant the sailing of invasion fleets which must have stimulated the demand for ropes. Taxation on hemp, flax and rope shows that it was a well-established industry by 1315.

In early Tudor times competition was encountered from foreign imports and from the neighbouring village of Burton Bradstock. This was unbearable, so a petition was sent to Henry VII stating that ruin faced the town, which had always made rope and was now being undercut by neighbouring villages over which there was no jurisdiction. Help came in 1530 with an Act that forbade the sale of hemp save in the Bridport market from an area of five miles thereabouts. No ropes were to be made elsewhere save for private use. This gave Bridport, for a time at least, a virtual monopoly of the Dorset rope production. Camden mentions that 'such tackle for the use of the English navy should be made nowhere else'. He may have seen agents bringing in the raw material from the farmers of West Dorset and the lands along the Fleet, watching it being weighed at the town beam and scales and sold to the manufacturers. He may have been told with pride that the hangman's ropes at Newgate were of Bridport make.

Despite the Act of 1530 other rope-walks were established in the naval dockyards of Deptford, Woolwich, Portsmouth and Plymouth; they began to use Dutch and Russian hemp which was as good as, if not better than the local product. Sea transport from Bridport was made difficult, since the harbour was silting up and road transport was uncertain. A new source of demand, however, stimulated the industry when the Newfoundland trade developed. Not only were ropes needed for this shipping, but the fishermen needed nets of different kinds and the industry had the initiative to make the change. By 1793 Claridge estimated that 1,800 people in the town and more than 7,000 in the neighbourhood were employed in making everything from very small nets to cables for men-of-war. Hutchins suggests even greater numbers at work.

Certainly the 1821 census shows that a fifth of all the Dorset families engaged in handicraft were to be found in Bridport.

The rope and net industry gave employment to all the family. Boys served an apprenticeship of ten or twelve years between the ages of seven and ten until twenty-one. As in other crafts, they could not marry during this time; parish overseers bound children to ropemaking as they did to silk-throwing in Sherborne or linen-making at Burton Bradstock. Other children, while not bound, also worked long hours turning the spinning-wheels or 'braiding' or netmaking along with their mothers. A little of this cottage industry is still to be found in the county. The children worked, according to Claridge, from 4 am to 9 pm if they were bound apprentices and from 6 am to 9 pm in summer and 7 am to 8 pm in winter if they lived at home.

When Claridge reported on Bridport there were a number of ropemakers, chief among them the firms of Hounsell and Gundry. The Gundrys owned a number of mills, the Court, the Grove and Pyemore. The stocktaking books of this concern, which deal with the years 1783–1803, show a diversified but very considerable business. The debts on the books stood at £10,372 9s 6d in 1795. In the following year the Navy bill alone was £249 12s. The weekly wage bills of the firm in the period 1807–15 might rise as high as £170. No longer was only local flax and hemp used; both were imported. In 1796 a letter to Philadelphia speaks of the price of hemp 'never so high before, tempestuous weather never equalled in this country . . . we are deprived of the supply of hemp [which] shipped in October was not received till now [February]. No manufacturer in this town had the smallest quantity by him.' Not only weather but war influenced prices. 'Till we have a peace it cannot be cheaper.' 'The price of Riga hemp is enormous . . . I lately paid £64 a ton . . . but the quality is excellent.' To ensure supplies during the blockade against Napoleon, Gundry took the precaution of ordering that his imported hemp should be put on board four different vessels in five separate lots. Claridge estimated that two-thirds of the flax and hemp used in Bridport was now imported from Europe and America.

The raw material was given to the combers for cleaning. It was then spun into twine on the wheels turned by the children and finally twisted on the broad rope-walks in front of the workers' houses. Boys turned the machines to which the thread was attached, while the men walked backwards along the walks drawing out the twisting threads. The rope had to be dried by being hung from hooks on the fronts of the workers' houses. From the factory the twine was sent out to the women to braid in their homes into nets of many kinds. The Gundry stocktaking book mentions seven kinds of seine nets, cod nets, rope nets, tannet nets, and white nets. In addition lines were listed with twine in the braiders' hands, also ropes, yarn, flax, hemp, carts, bags, wraps, oil and implements. Carpet thread was supplied to Kidderminster; shoe thread, bed cords, harness twine, sail twine, and good bleached canvas were all mentioned. For the seine nets corks had to be bought and lead weights were needed. Casks were used for packing; horses had to be hired and oats, hay and straw bought in addition to flax and hemp.

The extent of Gundry's trade as well as its variety is amazing. Letters go to Philadelphia, Baltimore, Boston, New York and Quebec dealing with ships out of London or Bristol. Gundry also appears to have undertaken commissions for his American buyers. One of his letters mentions a carpet being sent out in the *Polly* along with the salmon nets. A return cargo speaks of American horns being shipped to the Sheffield cutlers. 'The demand from the various parts of America is so great.' Goods went to Nova Scotia and Halifax for the Newfoundland fleets, to the Channel Islands and to Northern Ireland. The contracts with the Navy, which dated from 1728, continued. Goods supplied to the Commissioner of the Navy from May to December 1780 came to £387 1s 9d; from January to June 1782 £663 1s 9¾d. Round the fishing ports of the south coast went the Gundry travellers making what look like annual visits. One notebook gives twelve names of buyers at Dartmouth, fifteen at Portland, eleven at Brixham, eight at Teignmouth. From this last port goods were shipped by sea to Leith for Greenock and Glasgow, Poole was a point of embarkation for Liverpool, thence goods were dispatched to Manchester and Sheffield. Other trade was done with Christchurch, Lymington, Ringwood and the Dorset towns as well as with some inland Devon buyers. Harwich, Lowestoft and Margate on the east coast, and Milford Haven in Wales, all traded with Gundry. In 1808 the firm was enquiring about possible orders from Bremen and other north German ports.

To meet this flourishing trade Gundry seems to have bought

from fellow-ropemakers to resell. There are accounts with the firm of Hounsell, which had been established in 1670, and with Samuel Cox of Beaminster.

Unlike other Dorset industries, the rope and net concerns were able to make the transition from simple machinery and home hand labour to the more complex power-driven machinery of the later Industrial Revolution. Water-driven spinning machines were used by Willmott in his silk mills at Sherborne and by Roberts at Burton Bradstock. Weaving looms for sailcloth followed. By the middle of the nineteenth century ropemaking was becoming mechanized. Netmaking followed. In the present century new materials, nylon and terylene are used and a different range of goods has been developed at Bridport by an amalgamation of many small firms into Bridport Industries Ltd. Nylon in Bridport and glass fibre in Sherborne have ousted flax, hemp and silk.

*Cloth*

The West Country has been famous for its cloth at least from Tudor times. John Leland, who rode through the country in the fifteen-thirties, commented on the clothmakers of Wells and many 'pretty cloth making towns on the Cotswolds'. Fine broadcloth found a ready market at home and abroad. Many of the West Country clothiers were men of substance employing hundreds of cottage workers in Defoe's time. Although wool of fine quality was produced in Dorset, the cloth industry was never a really important one. Defoe praised the fine Spanish mixed cloth which he saw made in Sherborne, the master clothier sending out the wool for spinning and then collecting the yarn for the weavers.

In Dorchester there was a broadcloth industry in the early seventeenth century. William Blackford or Blachford, merchant clothier, exported almost half the cloth that left the county through Weymouth in 1625 for foreign ports, in the main to France. In 1609 Blackford, then aged about sixty, gave evidence about Dorset Dozens made, he said, of the coarsest sort of wool grown in the county. The finer wool was spun and sold in Wiltshire and Somerset to make fine broadcloth and fine Reading kerseys. The fine wool was sold for fourpence a pound, the coarser from twopence to threepence. A fleece of Dorset wool was usually spun into 300 reels and the Dozens were woven in 10–12-yard lengths, a yard in width, weighing almost the same number of pounds. Dorset Dozens could not compare with Devonshire Dozens for fineness. Blackford claimed that forty years previously little or no cloth was made in Dorset except linings, and that he was one of the first to introduce Dorset Dozens. Other witnesses in the enquiry were John Hitchecock of Broadwindsor, clothier, Walter Tuber and John Vyney, merchants of Lyme Regis, and Thomas Hooper, fuller of the same town. Other Dorset merchants also used the port for exporting Dorset kerseys, Somerset and Barnstaple bays, Gloucester small and broad cloth and other types as well. The Civil War disrupted the Dorchester industry; all Defoe could find was a little serge being made. Where woollen cloth was made at Lyme, Wareham, Bere Regis, Gillingham and Beaminster, it was hardly more than sufficient for local needs. By the eighteenth century Dorset had almost ceased to make up the local wools which were sent to neighbouring counties or to London. A little serge was still made in Beaminster till 1830 and sold at 1s 2d a yard.

One type of cloth, swan-skin, was produced throughout the eighteenth century in Shaftesbury and Sturminster Newton. This was a coarse white flannel used for soldiers' clothing and by the Newfoundland fishermen. In Sturminster in 1793 over a thousand hands were employed by four or five clothiers, the racks on which the cloth was fixed covering several fields. The cloth was made up in lengths of 35 yards selling at 1s 6d to 2s a yard. Up to 5,000 pieces a year were produced in Sturminster when the industry was at its height. It declined rapidly; Pigot's directory of 1830 gives only one manufacturer in the town.

The production of coarse linen, dowlais, in Gillingham and Cerne Abbas was on a modest scale, as was plain and striped cotton at Poole and Abbotsbury. A little serge was woven in the north at Stickland and linsey-wolsey was produced in Shaftesbury. The most important output of cloth came from Richard Roberts's linen mills at Burton Bradstock and from a group of sailcloth and sacking producers in Bridport and Beaminster. Roberts had a wide range of linen products, sheetings, hand-towels and wrappings. He made twine and cobblers' thread, cheese-cloth and canvas for bags. He was prepared to make bread-bags for the Navy, hop-bags for Worcestershire and mail-bags. At Burton some flax and hemp was grown by Roberts himself, some bought locally and some imported when war did not disrupt the trade with Scandinavia. The spinning, weaving and bleaching were all undertaken at Burton

Bradstock. Roberts was prepared to sell direct to shops or to fellow-merchants. He worked for Cox of Beaminster, and traded through agents in London to places throughout the West Country and in Northern Ireland. Like William Willmott, the silk spinner of Sherborne, Roberts used the new industrial inventions of his time, sending to the North of England for the best machinery available. The fact that neither Willmott nor Roberts were of Dorset stock may explain their more enterprising outlook. Roberts's sons lacked their father's ability and the enterprise came to an end.

The sailcloth industry mainly centred on Beaminster and Bridport, where Samuel Cox & Co had two large concerns. In the former town they employed 600 hands in 1793, with nearly 2,000 in the neighbourhood. In Bridport nearly 2,000 worked for the firm. The children got 2d or 3d for turning the spinning-wheels. They began to work when they were six or seven years old and started work at six in the morning, seven in the winter, till eight or nine at night. The women were paid 2d a pound for spinning: four pounds was an average day's work. The cloth was made up in 40-yard pieces and sold at 15d to 17d a yard. Four-bushel sacks for grain or flour from the same material cost 37s a dozen. There were still four sailcloth manufacturers in Bridport in 1830, but only two in 1842. Like the other Dorset industries, the techniques of mass production elsewhere had proved too competitive, together with the changing needs of nineteenth-century shipping.

## Buttons

Varieties of hand-made buttons seem to have been made in different parts of the county in the eighteenth century. Cloth buttons were made in Shaftesbury at the beginning of the century by Abraham Case. A flat disc of horn from the Dorset sheep was cut with a hole in the centre through which the cloth was pulled and then worked over with thread. A high button was produced for ladies' dresses and a polished flat one or a worked flat linen one for other clothes. Later in the century a wire button was developed. The work was done mainly by women in the cottages and brought to collecting-points where agents picked it up. Every Friday an agent was to be found at Milborne St Andrews. The brass wire for the ring frame came from Birmingham, and it was no doubt collected by the women bringing in their bundles of mites, birds' eyes, spangles, shirt, waistcoat and outsize buttons. As in other cottage industries the children helped with the work. Indeed, it was considered a desirable employment. Lady Caroline Damer, in her charity school for poor children, wished them to be instructed in button-making. The inhabitants of Blandford workhouse, men and women, were making considerable quantities. In one month, June 1770, three men and eleven women made fifteen gross of large and small buttons.

By the end of the eighteenth century Claridge, the contemporary surveyor, believed that four thousand women and children were employed round Shaftesbury, mainly by Mr Atchinson, who supplied the wire while the workers furnished the thread. He, too, trained children, paying them 1d a day until they were reasonably skilful and 1s a week thereafter. The women were paid by the gross, getting 1s 6d to 4s for the better kinds of button and 5d or so for inferior kinds. An expert worker could produce up to seven dozen buttons in a day. Among the Blandford workers, John Jenkins produced ten dozen on some days. There is the tantalizing note in the workhouse accounts that ten dozen buttons were lost by Hannah Elott 'while in her fits of folly'. She could hardly have swallowed so many. In addition to the workhouse button-makers there were several thousand home workers employed by Fisher & Co. So skilful were some of the girls and women that they found it more profitable to spend their time making buttons than working in the fields. Even if part of the wages were paid in goods they preferred this work. The children made the wire rings on a spindle according to the size of the button and soldered the ends together, the stringers counted and threaded the buttons into lots of 144, and the women and girls worked the various thread patterns, cross wheel, spider web and the like. The buttons were finally sewn on to different coloured papers according to their quality.

Shaftesbury and Blandford were the chief centres for the button trade, but it was also carried on in Bere Regis for a time and Hutchins mentions ring buttons and the sugar loaf made by women and children in Sturminster Newton. The trade was still flourishing in 1830. Pigot's directory gives four makers of shirt buttons, all in the Market Place in Blandford, and six agents for wire buttons in Shaftesbury. But the trade was declining. There is only one name given in the 1842 directory in place of ten. The development of the button machine completed the decline of this cottage industry which, in its heyday, had sent buttons from the villages to the collecting depots, thence to London where the firm of Case did business with Europe, Canada and New Zealand.

### *Stockings*

A smaller industry which has also ended was that of stocking-making, centred round Wimborne and Poole, with a small number of workers at Corfe Castle and others at Stalbridge. While Poole made silk stockings, those produced at Wimborne were knitted woollen ones for which the workers got 3s 6d to 4s a pair. When Defoe visited the county in the early part of the eighteenth century he commented that the Stalbridge trade was already decaying by reason of competition from the 'stocking engine or frame which has destroyed the hand knitter and put an end to the finest best highest prized in England'. The Wimborne worsted stockings survived into the nineteenth century. Each pair contained eight ounces of wool which cost twopence an ounce. At the height of the trade over a thousand men and women were employed in Wimborne, according to Claridge. The last stocking frames were broken up at the end of the nineteenth century.

### *Lace*

Here, too, the story is the same. In the seventeenth century lace was made at Blandford and Sherborne. Defoe considered the Blandford bone lace as fine as any in England. 'I never saw better in Flanders France or Italy.' This trade had ended by 1811, but in Lyme Regis in the eighteenth century almost every house in Broad Street was inhabited by a lacemaker who sat working at her door in summer. Queen Charlotte had a dress of Lyme Regis lace, but no Dorset lace could be found when Queen Adelaide wanted some.

### *Gloves*

Buttons, lace and stockings all failed in the face of machine competition; gloving, however, another cottage industry, survived. It was in origin older than the other crafts, being carried on in Bridport in the fifteenth century. Later the industry seems to have moved to Sherborne, Beaminster, Blandford, Cerne Abbas and Bere Regis. It is possible that the Dorset glovers were in fact middlemen acting as agents for at least one Yeovil manufacturer. At the beginning of the nineteenth century William Bidel, Yeovil glover, was buying from George Tucker of Beaminster, John

# Industries

Gouger of Sherborne and Thomas Bennett of Blandford. Gouger was a silk-thrower who may have been supplying material for gloves rather than gloves themselves; Thomas Hodges Bennett, of Salisbury Street, Blandford, was a linen and woollen draper and maker of buttons. Evidence given by William Willmott supports the belief that Dorset gloves were made for the Somerset industry which still exists.

## Paper

In the eighteenth century there were paper mills in and around Wimborne, Wareham and Beaminster. George Rogers was making paper at Wimborne in 1732. He was buying old rope and rags from Poole and also coal. Pigot's directory for 1830 mentions two paper-makers, George Hatchen of Walsford Mill and Henry Small at White Mill. A mill existed in East Street, Beaminster, in 1742.

Half a mile west of Wareham, on the Piddle, Robert Bacon occupied West Mills in 1753. This mill continued to work until 1830. Carey Mill, further west, was leased by Nathaniel Bond to Samuel Snelgar and Anthony Berryman in 1752. Here was one water-wheel, one beater, a press and a vat. In 1810 Joseph Mould leased the mill.

Another paper mill, at Witchampton on the River Allen, has had a longer working life. In the eighteenth century it had one or two vats for hand-made paper from linen and cotton rags, discarded sailcloth and rope. Here the Burt family has made paper for six generations. In 1791 Stephen Burt, paper maker, was at work. William Burt in 1840 employed forty hands. The Witchampton Paper Mills still exist.

## Other industries

Other trades such as brewing, pipe-making and rough pottery have had a limited life. Mention has already been made of the clay-cutting round Corfe Castle and the link with the Wedgwood Potteries. In Roman times there were kilns in the area. White clay was used for pipe-making. Coarse clay for brick-making was and still is used in the Poole area. Floor and wall tiles were developed in the mid-nineteenth century. The coarse domestic pottery is no longer made at Beaminster, but the finer Poole ware is now sent all over the country and abroad. Weymouth and Cerne Abbas beer

# Industries

must have been good, since the Sherborne manufacturers used to bring it by road for their personal use.

On the Brit there was a small shipbuilding yard which built some men-of-war in the nineteenth century. Other small industries such as stays, tape, ribbons and band strings had a purely local existence. Through the ages, as today, Dorset has been primarily an agricultural county.

# CHAPTER THIRTEEN

## *Agriculture and the agricultural labourer*

W hen the Tudor geographer Camden visited Dorset
he wrote with pleasure of its fruitful soil and of the
green hills where great numbers of sheep fed. The
Stuart geographers, Speed and Leigh, also spoke of the large flocks
to be seen in the county. Thomas Gerard of Trent noted the hills
'all overspread with innumerable flocks of sheep for which it
yields very good and sound feeding and from which the county
hath reaped an unknown gain'. Dorset sheep were thus important
in the seventeenth century. The sheep grazed on the hills by day
and were folded at night. Across the chalk ridge of the north and
down to Dorchester and Winfrith the flocks fed where the turf was
sweet and juicy. In winter the hill flocks of the north were sent down
into Blackmore Vale. Sometimes hay was fed in open racks as well.
William Ellis in his *Shepherd's Guide*, published at the end of the
eighteenth century, was enthusiastic about the care lavished on the
young lambs. He found the Dorset Horn hardy and docile and
capable of living on scant pasture. The mutton was excellent and
the fleece of fine wool weighed four pounds.

Whether Ellis had ever seen the pure Dorset breed is uncertain.
Many farmers had crossed their flocks to improve the size, which
was small. Certainly the mutton was much enjoyed. William Willmott, the Sherborne manufacturer, sent it away as presents. He
may well have visited the great local fair for the sale of the lambs.
Claridge was interested to find that the ewes were put to the rams
in the last week in April and lambing came in mid-September. The
ewes had reached the fair at Weyhill, Hampshire, a fortnight
earlier, some dropping their lambs on the road. In order to have
young meat ready for the Christmas table, the lambs bought at
Weyhill might be brought up in the farmhouses. Ewes that
lambed later provided 'grass lambs' which were fed on the spring

grass of the home counties. The Dorset breed were known to lamb twice a year.

The lambs were generally shorn in midsummer. Although Claridge praised the good quality of the wool, it was not as fine as that of other breeds. He believed that up to five pounds of wool could be shorn from a three-year-old ewe: this was probably an exaggeration. He estimated that there were 800,000 sheep, of which 150,000 were sold annually. Indeed in his survey the greatest proportion of land was pasture for sheep, 50,000 acres of water-meadow and 290,000 of ewe leas and downs, with more pasture and tillage where the ewes might be sent to winter. This seems to have been the peak of Dorset sheep-farming. Figures for the nineteenth century show a decline to 300,000 in 1900. It is only within recent years that the flocks are returning in any number to the hills.

Sheep-farming was all-important, Claridge found, with pioneer work being done in improved breeding. In contrast, agriculture generally was backward.

In Tudor and Stuart times there had been enclosure of lands in Dorset. Patches were reclaimed from the woods and waste and there was encroachment on the open fields too. The more fertile areas may have been temporarily enclosed even earlier and then gradually become permanent. Evidence from field names suggests this development. The lighter soil was enclosed, leaving the 'open and unenclosed parts generally in poor land'.

Claridge found a four-course system of wheat, barley or beans, oats and fallow being followed in the Blackmore enclosed lands. Ploughing he considered careless and insufficient; the lines were crooked, the plough large and heavy, drawn by four horses or six oxen in yoke. He strongly advocated that the Norfolk two-horse wheel plough and the Norfolk crop rotation should be adopted. There seemed to him to be little manuring, and bean seeds, for example, were broadcast and not drilled. There was no attempt to hoe. Arthur Young confirmed that, while there were some large farms where heavy liming was followed, the average yield from the county was under the national average and 'Dorset farmers crept along humble paths chalked out by Slovens of yore'. Apart from sheep-farming, the best management was in the care of the water-meadows which were carefully flooded from irrigation channels in the early spring and at later periods, with a good crop of hay resulting as a winter food. Here real care was shown in land drainage.

While sheep were most important, there was dairying in the Blackmore Vale and round Bridport and small dairies were noted by Claridge all over the county. He found a system unknown elsewhere whereby the farmers let out cows at a fixed price to the dairyman of from £3 to £8. The cream, turned into butter, found a market in Poole or, salted in tubs, as far away as Portsmouth and London. Skimmed milk made inferior cheese which was consumed locally. Claridge believed that this letting out of large numbers of cows did not promote a spirit of improvement. William Marshall, a contemporary of Claridge, was harsh in his condemnation of the Bridport grassland which badly needed drainage and where 'nutritious and more profitable herbage' should be sown instead of weeds and grasses.

Some cattle in the Dorchester area, Derbyshires and Leicestershires, were kept for beef, though they seem to have been dual-purpose. The Devon red oxen gave the 'finest grained meat in the kingdom'. Oxen from the county were sold in the London cattle markets. William Kaines sent some there; at home cattle sales were held in Stalbridge every fortnight. Claridge found little good to say of the horses in the county: 'The Dorset farmers pay little attention to shape, size or symmetry.'

Improvements, probably encouraged by high war prices, came to the county at the turn of the eighteenth century. When Stevenson reported in 1812 he found that the Norfolk rotation was being introduced. Turnips had appeared and the fallow field was disappearing, at least in the Blackmore Vale; 'the cultivation [of potatoes] has extended very rapidly and appears likely to be further increased'. Copyhold tenure had been declining all through the eighteenth century, giving place to the usual lease for ninety-nine years or three lives.

Mention has already been made of the early enclosure of waste, woodland and some common fields. The eighteenth century was to see the extension of this consolidation by exchange or by outright purchase of strip lands. By mutual arrangement compact buildings and enclosed fields were taking the place of large open fields. By the time enclosure by Act of Parliament was fashionable much of the arable land had acquired its modern pattern, so that the Acts often dealt only with the common and waste, all that remained. For example, at Corscombe only the pasture and waste were dealt with when 108 acres had to be reallocated.

The earliest enclosure by Act of Parliament in the county was that of Buckland Newton which dated from 1733, the last East Stoke Common in 1868, the greatest number coming during the period of the wars. Here changes were made by private Acts relating each to a specific parish, but other changes came under two general nineteenth-century Acts. Appeals allowed to Quarter Sessions in five out of sixty-nine awards show that the Commissioners who were dealing with the reallocation of land were guilty of some irregularity in procedure. This is not enough to suggest that the Commissioners were harsh in their arrangements. There is not sufficient evidence to say if they were prejudiced in favour of one class of landowners. In the case of the appeals to Quarter Sessions the appellants were not the chief landowners. There was no abrupt change from open to enclosed farming. At Winterbourne Monkton enclosure was completed within one year, but this was rare. Awards might be made nine or ten years after parliamentary sanction to enclose had been secured. Indeed, the Acts often authorized voluntary agreements of an earlier period. The Act of Bere Regis came late in 1846, but there were compact holdings there in 1775, some carved out of the open fields and others from the heath and woodland. Here and there the open fields lasted on until the beginning of the present century, and the hiring fairs described by Hardy were still within living memory then.

Large estates and fine manor houses graced the county. There were improving landlords like Lord Portman at Bryanston, the Framptons of Moreton and Humphrey Sturt at Crichel who carried out experiments with vetches, tree-planting, rabbit-control and heath reclamation. Sturt used steam power for threshing, as did Frampton at Moreton. Some new farmhouses may have been built in the nineteenth century. Landlords and tenant farmers with capital improved by drainage, manuring and the introduction of new grasses. Machines for threshing, grinding and chaff-cutting were introduced. Lord Portman used a milking pound drawn from place to place by the dairyman's horse enabling the muck to be distributed over the land. Bones which had hitherto been sold were ground down for home use. By the mid-nineteenth century superphosphates and nitrate of soda were used as top dressing for the soil.

# Agriculture and the agricultural labourer

The coming of the railway stimulated the production of milk and butter for more distant markets, but other crops began to diminish. Baltic flax and hemp challenged and killed the Dorset crops. The sheep flocks fell in size as the nineteenth century progressed; the acreage under wheat shrank and fewer green crops were produced. No wonder the agricultural labourer, whose lot had not been easy, tried to better himself by joining a branch of Joseph Arch's Union. Changes in crops and husbandry did not always help the humbler folk.

## The agricultural labourer

When Stevenson published his *General View of the agriculture of the County of Dorset* in 1812 he was describing a rural society whose wages had shown little alteration over the years. There were parts of the county where money earnings were supplemented by an allowance of barley or wheat at a low and fixed price. In the Kingston Russell area, where labour was short, he noted 9s a week, a free cottage and fuel; at Abbotsbury a rate of 9s a week with house and fuel worth 3s. Elsewhere 8s in winter, 8s 6d in summer, with 14s at harvest-time, were paid. These rates reflect an improvement on the details which Sir F. M. Eden had collected in his 1797 *Survey of the State of the Poor*. In the neighbourhood of Blandford 6s in the winter months, 7s at other times were noted. Earnings may have improved over the turn of the century, but a background of war meant higher prices. The Dorset labourers lived mainly on wheaten or barley bread, skim milk, cheese, puddings, potatoes and other vegetables. The expenses of a Sherborne family of five in 1789 covered 3s for bread, 1½d for salt, 8d for meat, 7d for cheese, 2d for tea and 4d for milk, with a further outlay for soap. Candles and thread brought the total to 5s 8d for the week. Additionally, in the case of this family, there was rent to pay, fuel to be bought and £1 to be spent in the year on clothes. To cover this outlay the man earned 6s a week and his wife 2s 6d. This family may not have been a typical country one, but that of a town operative. A family of five ate a bushel of wheat a week. If they dared to make cakes, baking them on a gridiron, they were condemned as extravagant. If the women of the household drank tea they were criticized as squandering money on luxuries rather than on more substantial nourishment. They should have drunk the several pints of ale that the men enjoyed. But the illiterate women could not defend themselves against their detractors; if they justified themselves it must have been quietly. The evidence does not exist. Were they really so ignorant that, as reported, they scarcely knew how to wash and mend their own clothes? It is not surprising that, to the indignation of the farmers, when buttony was available the women preferred to earn 1s or 1s 6d rather than 9d weeding corn. It was said that they laid out the money in fine clothes, but this was a gibe made everywhere in England by the upper classes against those whom they felt were trying to better themselves.

For what was at best a meagre wage the Dorset labourers worked from six in the morning to nightfall at harvest-time, the women a little less. They might enjoy free ale or cider at a gallon a day and perhaps a little meat, the cheapest bits of bacon or 'legs and stickings at 3d a pound'. No wonder there was poaching. A recent investigation by Miss Barbara Kerr has shown that, compared with other counties, Dorset wages were low and the labourer was proverbially poor; 'indeed he and his family could hardly have survived but for poor relief and the practice of farmers to make allowances, either free or at reduced rates, of fuel and grist or coarsely ground corn'. As late as 1880, when the national average for agricultural work was 14s 1¾d, Dorset wages were only 11s. It is not surprising that men poached, stole and smuggled; if they were caught there was little mercy. After the end of the Napoleonic Wars more men were convicted of poaching, deer-stealing and attacks on keepers; they paid for their crime with transportation. There was thus need for the children to work as soon as they could to supplement the family earnings. A lad might earn 1s 6d as a birdscarer.

It is true that some labourers lived in free cottages, but these were scarce and overcrowding was terrible. In 1842 the Rector of Bryanston, giving evidence to the Poor Law Commissioners, described a cottage with only one bedroom thirteen feet square, containing three beds. On one lay the mother, a widow dying of consumption, in the next two daughters of eighteen and twelve, and in the third a young newly-married couple. The rector commented that illegitimate children were inevitable in such circumstances. One of the Poor Law Commissioners himself investigated a two-roomed cottage at Stourpaine. The only bedroom was ten feet by ten with one fifteen-inch square window. Here were three beds. In one slept father, mother and the two youngest children;

in the second three daughters—twins of twenty and one of seven; in the third were four boys between ten and seventeen. There was no curtain between the beds, no ceiling and the thatched roof was only seven feet high at the apex. This was an extreme case, but a single bedroom for the whole family was fairly general. It is not surprising that typhus was to sweep through the villages. Stevenson had believed that Dorset was a healthy county and quoted Dr Arbuthnot as saying that a physician could neither live nor die in Dorset. Ague was rife in the eighteenth century and typhus struck virulently. A Blandford doctor described a cottage where everyone had the disease. In two bedrooms were an old man and his wife, two middle-aged daughters, a son, his wife and three children. 'The son's wife and two of her children were on a bed in an out-house; in the outhouse was a well and a large tub containing pigs' victuals.' At Ryme Intrinsica the Reverend Sidney Osborne visited a labourer's home to find the wife with her two children eating bad potatoes and some bread, with a child lying dead in a coffin near them. The only entry to the bedroom was by a broken ladder; the rain poured through the broken roof on to the bed. Ashley Cooper wrote uneasily in his diary in 1843: 'Here I am in Quarter Sessions; the same vice the same misery—population increasing and crime also. The evil and the danger growing hand in hand and yet not an attempt at remedy.' A speech which Ashley made at a meeting of the Agricultural Society at Sturminster exasperated his father, who told him that the labourers did very well on six or seven shillings a week, he could not afford to build cottages and that Ashley was making mischief. Dorothy Wordsworth had earlier described cottages she had seen made from mud and scrapings from the roads. There was no money for clothing. At Affpuddle poverty was so great that there was nothing to spare. 'Clothes they get as they can and the children go nearly naked.'

The labourers had made one attempt, however, to remedy their impoverished conditions and what they regarded as a lowering of their status in society. This feeling was not peculiar to Dorset. The problem of village destitution had by the end of the 1790s passed beyond any solution that could be offered by an individual. Repression or palliatives, exhortations and sermons were of no avail; the labourers began to organize in a simple fashion. It is probable that they were encouraged by nonconformist clergy. The Church of England had failed; many parsons influenced the local administration of the Poor Law and appeared as the labourers' enemies. They were often connected with the local landowning families. Nonconformity gave scope for self-help and a share in church organization. In a number of Dorset villages there was a nonconformist chapel and the stirring sermons heard there certainly influenced some of the Dorset labourers who were to try to better their conditions by forming a branch of a trade union.

By 1830 the repressive sentences of the justices, the inadequacy of the Poor Law, the changes in agricultural methods and the pious attitude of those who preached humility and contentment with an intolerable lot brought matters to a head. A wave of rick-burning and machine-wrecking swept the south. In Kent and Essex in the summer of 1830 there were widespread attacks on landlords and clergy. In November fires burned in Sussex and deputations waited on the farmers to demand higher wages. The rising in Hampshire was marked by a considerable destruction of property. A cloth factory in Wiltshire was attacked. The tide of unrest reached Dorset. Lord Melbourne, the Home Secretary, wrote on 25 November to Okeden, one of the county magistrates who lived at More Crichel, expressing the hope 'that all magistrates will act with promptitude decision and resolution' to combat 'open acts of violence and secret and malicious destruction of property'. A promise of help from the Army and the coastguards 'to aid the civil powers on requisition of the magistrates' was made. The magistrates began to enrol a force of special constables. The Reverend Henry Syndecombe noted in his diary on 26 November, 'great alarm and apprehension in the immediate neighbourhood from the destruction of property near Dorchester', and next day, 'Gosforth dined with me after swearing in 116 persons to act as Constables for six months'. On 30 November thirty more were enrolled in the west of the county. A letter from E. B. Portman to Okeden spoke of 2,000 pedestrian constables ready to resist any mob and 200 armed and mounted men. There was a troop of Lancers at Blandford. Arrangements were made for a meeting to consider agricultural wages. Sir J. W. Smith, in a letter to Okeden, suggested 10s a week for the able bodied, 7s for boys of 16 to 20 and 3s 6d for the aged and infirm, though he feared that if the full allowance were to fall on the land-lords he did not know what would become of him.

At Moreton, near Dorchester, James Frampton began to pre-pare to defend his home. Frampton had earlier 'harangued the people at Bere Regis and argued with them on the impropriety of their conduct, refusing to concede to their demands whilst asked with menaces. This spirited conduct', said his sister, 'caused him to be very unpopular and there were threats against him'. A rick was fired at Broadmayne near by; Mary Frampton wrote in her Journal:

> Notice was received of an intending rising of the people at Winfrith, Wool and Lulworth . . . which took place on 30th. My brother Mr Frampton was joined early in the morning by a large body of farmers etc.—all special constables amounting to 150 armed only with short staff, the pattern of which had been sent by order of the Government. Numbers increased as they rode towards Winfrith where the clergyman was very unpopular and his premises supposed to be in danger. The mob urged on from behind the hedge by a number of women and children advanced rather respectfully and with hats in hands to demand an increase of wages but would not listen to a request that they should disperse. The Riot Act was read. They still urged forward and came up close to Mr Frampton's horse; he then collared the man but in giving him in charge he slipped from his captors by leaving his smock frock in their hands. Another mob from Lulworth was said to be advancing . . . the mob was described in general as very fine looking young men and particularly well dressed as if they had put on their best clothes for the occasion.

Mary Frampton relates how their home was barricaded, the women took it in turns to sit up at night and the Dorset militia men patrolled. No wonder this situation was compared with Ireland. While this unrest was revealing itself in the Dorchester, Bere Regis and Winfrith area there was trouble in the north of the county. With the help of the Lancers, Blackmore Vale was scoured and seventeen prisoners were taken, the rest of the mob dispersing. There is something ironic in the complaint of one Dorset land-owner that three gardeners refused to be sworn in as specials. While Frampton refused to make any concessions, others took their threshing-machines to pieces, stored them out of the way and granted increased wages. The Gillingham farmers agreed to a standard rate of 9s.

December opened with more fires, ricks of corn being destroyed near Stinsford. A description was circulated in the Blandford area of two fire-raisers; 'they are dressed like farmers, one a man of about 40 rides a long legged light carcassed sorrel coloured horse'.

The Dragoon Guards supported the Lancers. One threatening letter to Mr Castleman declared: 'Sunday night your house shall come down to the Ground for you are an inhuman monster and we will dash out your brains. Banks and your set ought to be sent to Hell. The Hanley Torches have not forgotten you.' Mr Murray, the clergyman at Stinsford, found a dirty rumpled paper threatening to burn his barn and ricks. He thought the note must have been thrust into his pocket. Men were captured and committed for trial from Hanley, Alderholt, Winfrith, Stour Provost, Iwerne Courtney, Shaftesbury, Stalbridge, Mappowder, East Stour, Wolland and Buckland Newton. No wonder Syndecombe could remark that 'the gaols were overfilled with the prisoners sent in'. The *Dorset County Chronicle* reported 200. And while the gaols filled the Frampton family unbarred their windows for Christmas and enjoyed peacock and a boar's head.

On 10 January 1831 the prisoners were tried by a Special Commission at Dorchester. Protection was afforded by 200 specials at 3s a day. Mr Justice Alderson opened the proceedings with a dissertation on the economics of machinery, the duties incumbent on the gentry who were bidden to discourage and discountenance, and if necessary to prosecute the dangerous publications that were doing so much harm in rural districts. They were to go home and educate their poorer neighbours.

> Poverty is indeed, I fear, inseparable from the state of the human race, but poverty itself and the misery attendant on it, would no doubt be greatly mitigated if a spirit of prudence were more generally diffused among the people and if they understood more fully and practised better their civil, moral and religious duties.

This cannot have brought any consolation to men like George Legg, waiting in the dock, who had tried to support a family of five children, without parish help, on 7s a week in a free cottage but without any free fuel. Many witnesses, including the parish clergyman, testified to Legg's exemplary character. In all, seventy-one men were convicted of rioting and breaking threshing-machines. Many were transported, 'sent', says Mary Frampton, 'to New Zealand and New Holland where their agricultural knowledge might be useful'. One was sentenced to transportation for life and eleven for seven years, others were sentenced to various terms of imprisonment and a few were acquitted. Sharp sentences, it was hoped, that would keep the labourers in submission for the future.

This hope was not immediately fulfilled. The farmers of the Puddletown area had agreed to a rise of wages to 10s a week. They shortly repented of their decision and began to reduce the pay. Writing in 1837, George Loveless tells how, when the wages were down to 8s:

> all the men in the village with the exception of two or three invalids, made application to a neighbouring magistrate, namely William Morton Pitt Esq of Kingston House, and asked his advice, he told us that if the labourers would appoint two or three and come to the county hall the following Saturday he would apprise the chief magistrate James Frampton . . . and at the same time our employers should be sent for to settle the subject.

Wages fell to 7s with notice that they would be further reduced.

> The labouring men consulted together what had better be done, as they knew it was impossible to live honestly on such scanty means. I had seen at different times accounts of Trade Societies; I told them of this and they willingly consented to form a friendly society among the labourers, having sufficiently learnt that it would be vain to seek redress either of employers magistrates or parsons.

Shortly afterwards two delegates from the Grand Nation Trade Union visited and gave directions. The two Loveless brothers then established the Friendly Society of Agricultural Labourers at Tolpuddle. For this village club the elaborate ritual and code of rules of the Grand Nation were adopted. No secrecy was observed, for John Loveless ordered from the village painter a figure of 'a complete skeleton on a dark ground six feet high and over the head "Remember thine end" '. This was used to make the initiation ceremony more impressive. More than forty labourers joined. Witnesses later confirmed that in the house of one of the accused, Thomas Stanfield, James Loveless in a white dress 'not a smock frock' read from what seemed to be the Bible and from certain rules that a shilling entrance fee should be paid, with a penny a week subscription. Those being initiated were blindfolded. Alarmed by this, the farmers induced the local magistrate, on 21 February 1834, to issue placards warning the labourers that membership of a union would be deemed a felony with liability to seven years' transportation. This was no idle threat; within three days the Lovelesses and four others were in gaol.

In March the trial opened. The men had neither struck nor presented an application for higher wages. They had neither used threats nor committed any outrage worse than administering oaths. 'Suffice it to say, the most unfair and unjust means were resorted to in order to frame an indictment against us; the grand jury appeared to ransack heaven and earth to get some clue against us.' There was no testimony that the six labourers were anything but honest, sober men. Out of the ordinary, perhaps, in that two at least were Methodist lay preachers. The judge nevertheless charged the grand jury as if treason or murder had been committed. After a brief trial the labourers were sentenced to seven years' transportation under an Act of 1797, passed after the naval mutinies, against illegal oath-taking. Lord Melbourne expressed the opinion that 'the law has been in this case most properly applied'. Contrary to usual practice, the prisoners were sent to the hulks before March was ended, and were on the high seas bound for Australia before the middle of April. By the time petitions could be presented the Tolpuddle labourers were safely out of the country. The importance of the trial of the labourers, which took place in the Old Shire Hall in Dorchester in a court room preserved today as a memorial, far outstripped local history. For a time it crushed the growth of trade unionism. Although the Grand Nation immediately discontinued all initiation ceremonies, the fear of the law drove many workers out of the movement and helped to ensure its collapse. Only in 1836 were the Tolpuddle labourers pardoned and allowed to return to England. A fund was raised to resettle them on farms. George Loveless published his *Victims of Whiggery* and subsequently, with four of his fellows, emigrated to Canada, but not before he had taken a small part in the Chartist Movement. To a convention held in 1839 at the Bristol Hotel, Cockspur Street, London, Loveless was nominated as the sole representative of a rural area. He did not, however, sit. The chapel where Loveless preached stands in Tolpuddle with a row of cottages on the hill built a century later as a memorial to the six 'Tolpuddle Martyrs'.

Years later the school log-book of Woodsford reveals the exclusion of some labourers from the village because they had joined a union in the seventies.

The Dorset labourer continued to face a life of low wages and overcrowded cottages. Because of changes in Poor Law administration he could no longer hope for outdoor relief. Village industries were waning, so that extra money could not be expected. Poverty marked the villages of the barren heathlands, the compact villages and the scattered farmsteads alike. The population grew steadily to make matters worse. Though there were village schools, children were withdrawn to work at an early age. The men had neither spirit nor the equipment to seek work elsewhere. Dorset agricultural wages continued to be among the lowest in the country. The depression at the end of the nineteenth century, better transport and a more progressive attitude finally forced many Dorset labourers to leave their home villages for work elsewhere.

# Bibliography

GENERAL

Hutchins. *History and Antiquities of the County of Dorset.* John Bowyer Nichols, 1861–70.

Leland. *Itinerary* 1745.

Camden. *Britannia* 1806.

Defoe. *Tour through the whole Island.* Peter Davies, 1927.

Claridge, J. *General View* 1793.

Stevenson, W. *General View of the Agriculture of the County* 1812.

*Victoria County History.* Constable, 1908.

Foster, J. J. *Wessex Worthies.* Dickinsons, 1920.

*Proceedings and Transactions of Dorset Natural History and Archaeological Society*: abbreviated as *Proceedings*.

*Notes and Queries for Somerset and Dorset*: abbreviated as *Somerset and Dorset*.

Dorset Year Books.

CHAPTER I

Bankes, V. *A Dorset Heritage.* Richards Press, 1953.

Saunders, Lloyd. *Patron and Place Hunter.* Lane, 1919.

Dodington, Bubb, *Diary* 1749 and 1784.

Weymouth Corporation Records: Council Minute Book C and Sherren Papers.

County Records: Inventories.

CHAPTER 2

Weymouth Corporation Records.

State Papers Domestic. Public Records Office.

Acts of Privy Council.

Stowe MSS, British Museum.

Munster Rolls.

County Records, KS 17, 9249, KQ1, 11730, NZ/G1.

# Bibliography

*Somerset and Dorset.* Vol xx.
*Proceedings.* Vol xi, xli.


CHAPTER 3

Frampton, Mary. *Journal*, ed. Mundy, H. G. Sampson Low, 1885.
Ham, Elizabeth, ed. Gillett, E. Faber & Faber, 1944.
Ellis, G. A., *History of Melcombe Regis.* Benson, 1829.
Burney, Fanny. *Diary.* Dent, 1940.
Delmotte. *Weymouth Guide.* 1785.
*Somerset and Dorset.* Vol xxi.
Bower, A. C. MSS letters. County Records.
*Dorchester and Sherborne Journal.*


CHAPTER 4

*Paston Letters.* Dent, 1910.
Scott, E. *King in Exile.* Constable, 1905.
*Review of English Studies.* Vol. viii. Oxford.
Wordsworth, Dorothy. *Letters*, ed. Knight, W. A. Boston & London, 1907.
*Salisbury and Winchester Journal.*
Dorset Year Book, 1959/60.


CHAPTER 5

Hutchins, *Corfe.*
Puddletown MSS Records.
Melbury. County Records. 136/21.


CHAPTER 6

*Sherborne Journal.*
County Records. Calendar of Prisoners. 10945.
Shore, H. N. *Smuggling days and smuggling ways.* Allen, 1892.
Hardy, W. M. *Smuggling days in Purbeck.* Dorset County Chronicle, 1907.
*Somerset and Dorset.* Vol xviii.
Dorset Year Book, 1959/60.
Roberts, G. *Social History of the People of the Southern Counties.* Longmans, 1856.

# Bibliography

CHAPTER 7

Manuscript books of Willmott, Pretor and Roberts. County Records.

Pinney Papers, now in Bristol University.

CHAPTER 8

County Records.

CHAPTER 9

County Records.

Metropolitan Commissioners Report 1844; 1847.

Hunter, R. and MacAlpine, I. *Three hundred years of Psychiatry.* Oxford, 1963.

Jones. K. *Lunacy Law and Conscience.* Routledge, 1950.

CHAPTER 10

County Records. Diaries of Maria Carter.

Account book of Stephens & Reynolds.

CHAPTER 11

Fowler, J. *Medieval Sherborne.* Longmans (Dorchester), 1951.

Wagner, A. F. H. V. *Gillingham Grammar School.* Blackmore Press, 1958.

Select Committee on Education of the Poor.

Endowed Charities, Brougham Commissions.

Mayo, C. H. *Municipal Records of the Borough of Dorchester.* Pollard & Co, 1908.

Dorset Year Book 1959/60.

Clegg, A. L., *Wimborne Grammar School.* Outspoken Press, 1960.

*Proceedings.* Vol xxviii.

*Somerset and Dorset.* Vol xvii.

School Log Books.

CHAPTER 12

*Somerset and Dorset.* Vols xxv, xxvi, xv, xlii, xxxv.

*Proceedings.* Vols xiii, lxx, lix.

Hudson, K. *Industrial Archaeology of Southern England.* David & Charles, 1965.

County Records D 128/B1, P 70/OV 33, D 203.

# Bibliography

CHAPTER 13

Hammond, J. L & B. *Village Labourer*. Longmans, 1911.
Webb, S. & B., *History of Trade Unionism*. Longmans, 1900.
*Proceedings*. Vols xxxii, lxxiii, lxxvii, lxxxii, lxxxiv.
Eden, Sir F. M. *State of the Poor*. 1797.
Young, Arthur. *The Farmer's Tour*. 1771.
*Dorset County Chronicle*.

The date given is of the edition used, which may not always be that of the earliest publication.

# *Acknowledgements*

The author gratefully acknowledges the help given to her by Miss M. Holmes, Dorset County Archivist and Mr R. Peers of the Dorchester Museum. Mrs O. K. Collett kindly did the line-drawings in the text and Mr R. R. Sellman prepared the two maps. The Gillray cartoon, plate number 4, is in the possession of the proprietor of the Gloucester Hotel, Weymouth. Plates numbers 10, 11 and 15 have been reproduced by kind permission of the Royal Commission on Historical Monuments (England), number 18 through the courtesy of the Trade Union Congress; the pictures of the old silk mill and rope works by permission of Mr Kenneth Hudson. Mr C. D. Baker helped with the preparation of the illustrations, Miss P. Havord typed the manuscript which Mr John Tetley did much to improve. To all these the author gives her thanks.

# Index

*Plates are indicated in bold*

# Index

# Index

# Index

# Index